ALSO BY MARION CUNNINGHAM

The Fannie Farmer Cookbook
(Thirteenth Edition)

The Breakfast Book

The Fannie Farmer Baking Book

The Fannie Farmer Cookbook
(Twelfth Edition)
(with Jeri Laber)

THESE ARE BORZOI BOOKS
PUBLISHED IN NEW YORK BY ALFRED A. KNOPF, INC.

THE SUPPER BOOK

Marion Cunningham

THE
SUPPER
BOOK

Illustrated by Donnie Cameron

Alfred A. Knopf · New York ·

To Rover, who cleans his
supper bowl every night

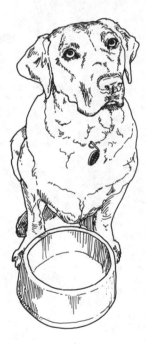

Acknowledgments

This book has had the benefit of many friends who have gener-. ously given wise advice and wonderful supper recipes. My deepest thanks to:

Michael Bauer	Bill Staggs
John Goyak	Fritz Streiff
Sharon Kramis	Susan Subtle
Loni Kuhn	Sherry Virbila
Mary Peacock	

A special word of appreciation to Donnie Cameron for her great Rover drawings, and to Judith Jones, always a fine friend and editor.

Contents

Introduction

I love supper. The idea of supper always conjures up a simple, easy, flexible meal marked by the intimacy of family or friends. Or it is sometimes enjoyed blessedly alone. Sitting down to one dish, with bread, butter, and a dessert, can put the world back into a pleasant perspective.

If ever we needed supper back in favor, it is today. A one-dish meal can solve a lot of problems for almost everyone. It is a godsend for beginning cooks and for those who work away from home—which is just about everyone today.

The whole concept of supper is to use things that you have on hand, both standard shelf items and foods that keep well refrigerated, such as eggs, mayonnaise, cheese, carrots, celery, maybe a cabbage, some iceberg lettuce, apples, pears, and other fruits in season. Then you don't have to stop on the way home and buy the makings for a whole dinner. Many of my supper recipes, you'll find, are created with what's likely to be found in your own kitchen, if you've done some thinking ahead and replenished your stock when you shop.

In addition, a good number of the recipes are a meal in a casserole, and they often benefit from mellowing overnight in the refrigerator. Recently "fresh and fast" has become the cook's creed, but preparing a mixture of ingredients in one dish and letting it cook in the oven can produce great savory food with a depth and richness of flavor that "fresh and fast" doesn't achieve. Spanish *Riso*, Holey Moley Tamale Pie, and Applesauce Lamb Curry are all good examples of dishes that can be prepared ahead at some leisurely moment. They simply need reheating and they are ready, without any last-minute fuss, to go into action and provide a whole meal for whoever comes home hungry and impatient to eat.

In the past we have relegated soups and salads to first courses or side dishes, but why shouldn't they make ideal main dishes when the servings are ample? A flavorful, substantial soup like Chicken Custard in Broth, or a salad like Buffalo Chicken Wing Salad, or Posole Salad Soup, a dish that combines both salad and soup, makes a wonderful supper dish that is so much more inviting in the evening than the typical lamb chop, peas, and potato kind of dinner. And so much more interesting. I have drawn from many of the ethnic influences that are surfacing all around the country today to achieve bolder accents and a nice blending of flavors in these good earthy dishes with humble origins.

In a chapter I call "Fringe Dishes," I have offered some easy-to-prepare accompaniments to enliven simple fare, such as rice infused with jasmine (you just crush the contents of a tea bag into the cooking water) and store-bought rolls warmed and drizzled with garlic, parsley, and oil, which taste better than you can imagine. Also in this chapter are condiments that can be made in minutes on a rainy Sunday and preserved by refrigeration. A few pickles, a relish, a colorful salsa, or a crunchy slaw can transform a meal, and it's nice to be able to put a tempting bowl on the table to sharpen the flavors and textures of dishes for those who like bolder tastes.

Supper without something sweet wouldn't be complete for me. It may be as elementary as persimmons with maple syrup and cream, or a half a peach on a piece of sugared toast, or a soothing wine jelly, all of which you'll find in the dessert chapter. But if you don't have time to prepare anything, a plate of broken-up pieces of chocolate served with coffee can be a surprisingly good treat. That offering of a little bit of chocolate instead of making a dessert reminds me of how much we miss if we think we have to serve a fancy dinner every time we invite someone over for a meal. Actually there are two schools of thought on this subject. One camp believes firmly that you do honor to guests, particularly if they've been invited in advance, by making something special and serving a full-course dinner with all the frills; just giving them potluck is somehow insulting, as though you couldn't bother to make the extra effort. The other camp—the one to which I belong—feels that sharing the family meal is a privilege, that there is something deeply satisfying about sitting down and partaking of just what would be ordinarily served in that home. In fact, it is often a relief to feel that the host hasn't spent hours in the kitchen and that the food, as long as there is enough of it, isn't something special. (I exclude, of course, holidays, birthdays, or a dinner for a visiting dignitary.) My argument is that during the last twenty or thirty years, with almost every adult working away from home, there has been a shortage of time, energy, and money too, for us to go all out to impress guests. But when you ask them to "come for supper," the expectation will be for a more scaled-down and intimate meal.

Supper is more a state of mind than a meal bound by rules. Above all, it shouldn't be prepared watching the clock and racing through all the cooking. Nothing destroys the pleasure and natural rhythm of kitchen work so quickly. The kitchen should be a soothing place, especially after a hectic day in the work world. Cooking supper for yourself and others can be a welcome change of thought and tempo. It can be one of the nicest times of the day.

THE SUPPER BOOK

Supper Salads

California Caesar Salad

Spinach Salad with Chutney Dressing

Green Rose Salad

Asparagus Salad

Potato Salad

Waldorf Salad

Avocado and Bacon Salad

Salmon Salad Niçoise

Tuscan Bean and Tuna Salad

Mustard Ring Salad

Buffalo Chicken Wing Salad

Beef Salad with Sour Pickles

U ntil not too long ago, Americans considered salads sissy food. Today salads are a symbol of health and nutrition, and salad bars are one of the biggest food businesses in this country. What is a salad? My definition is any greens, herbs, vegetables, or other foods, cooked or uncooked, that are served cold or at room temperature, with a dressing. Salads make ideal supper dishes, but they need a little heft to be satisfying. No matter how big a bowl of greens you serve, it won't suffice unless substantial fringe dishes are served, too.

Beware of the notion that salad can be made by tossing together a hodgepodge of ingredients in a bowl and then calling it a day. Turning out a splendid salad takes as much attention as braising fish. If greens are used, be ready to discard the coarse blemished leaves. Wash away all grit and dry the leaves thoroughly, because dressing won't adhere to water. Put the leaves in a plastic bag with a dampened paper towel and store in the refrigerator until chilled and ready to use. Carefully look over all your salad ingredients, and discard any cooked vegetables that are soggy or mushy. Cooked meats, chicken, fish, and shellfish must be carefully trimmed and fresh-tasting.

The dressing of salad is critical: how you make it and how you apply it. The most common dressing is vinaigrette, oil and acid blended, with a variety of other flavors often added. The acid is usually lemon or other citrus, or vinegar. The most popular oil used today is olive. Buying an olive oil you like is sometimes diffi-cult. Money does not necessarily buy the best, and the labels of extra virgin, extra fine, and so on only confuse the issue. Use a robust olive oil for rustic, hearty salads and a fine, subtle olive oil for delicate salads. The only way you find an olive oil that pleases you is by tasting a variety of them. I don't know of any shortcuts to doing this.

A vinaigrette must be properly balanced. One of the most com-mon errors is to use so much acid that the dressing tastes over-whelmingly sour and all the good qualities of the salad are lost. The old standard rule for making vinaigrettes was three parts oil to one part acid; this makes a far too acid mixture for most palates. You will notice that in some of my vinaigrettes, I have cut the dressing with a few spoonfuls of water, which makes it lighter and smoother. We are now back to my best basic rule for all cooking: taste as you make, and add only a little of whichever of the four basic taste-makers you are using. (They are sweet, sour, salty, or bitter.) Trust your own palate, and remember, to be a good cook you must be in control of the recipe you are making by critically tasting. This rule applies to everything you prepare.

A green salad should be dressed just before serving. Be careful to add only enough dressing to coat the leaves. Add a little at a time and toss gently until all leaves have a sheen. It is easy to overdo the dressing and end up with salad soup. Salads such as potato, chicken, fish, or other seafood should be dressed well before serv-ing so the flavors can blend and mellow. Then taste and correct the salt and pepper just before serving, because this type of salad seems to become bland after a few hours of chilling. It is also important to add only enough creamy dressing to make a moist salad: it should be neither dry nor sodden.

I want you to try the Buffalo Chicken Wing Salad (see page 20); it is just the ticket for a supper picnic, with lots of fire, crunch, and flavor. The Waldorf Salad (see page 14) with applesauce dressing is better by far than the traditional version, and the Caesar Salad (see page 8) in the classic California style is easy to make and will get lots of good comments.

SAYING GRACE

Saying a prayer before supper is a custom common to all cultures and all religions that is probably as old as the human race. Gratitude is a basic human feeling and it is natural to have shared ways of asking for blessing, giving thanks, or remembering others. Many of us have heard a solemn grace said over a holiday turkey, but saying grace can also be as simple as saying "Enjoy your meal!"

I have been asking friends and acquaintances if they say grace and I have been glad to hear that many do (on special occasions, at any rate). Saying grace before supper can be a ritual of fellowship that reminds us that we're at the table for more than just the food.

California Caesar Salad

(four servings)

This is called a California Caesar Salad because it's a variation on the original salad invented by Caesar Cardini, a Tijuana restaurateur in the 1930s who had a ritzy Hollywood clientele. For a perfect Caesar salad, it's essential to use only the crisp, tender inner leaves of romaine lettuce.

4 slices homemade-style bread
3 tablespoons olive oil

2 heads romaine lettuce

Dressing
½ cup olive oil
3 cloves garlic
2 tablespoons lemon juice, or
   to taste
½ teaspoon salt

5 anchovy fillets, or to taste
   (start with just 3 anchovies
   and taste, adding more if
   desired)

1 ounce Parmesan cheese,
   freshly grated (⅓ cup)

To make croutons, preheat the oven to 250°F. Cut the slices of bread into cubes, first removing the crusts. Spread the bread cubes out on a baking sheet, and put in the oven for about 12 minutes, or until the bread is dried out. Heat the 3 tablespoons olive oil in a frying pan over medium heat, add the bread cubes, and fry them, turning frequently, until all sides are golden brown. Remove from the heat and reserve.

Separate the leaves from the heads of romaine lettuce, then wash and dry them. Discard the dark, coarse outer leaves and any that are wilted or blemished. The presentation of the salad is more attractive when the leaves are left whole, although it is more manageable to eat when they are cut into bite-size pieces—the choice is up to you.

Put the olive oil and garlic in a blender and blend until smooth and creamy. Add the lemon juice and the salt and mix. Pour the dressing into the bottom of a large salad bowl. Add the anchovy fillets to the bowl and mash them into the oil mixture until well blended. Put in the romaine leaves and toss until all the leaves are coated and shiny. Add the croutons and toss lightly to mix. Sprinkle the cheese over the salad just before serving.

Spinach Salad with Chutney Dressing

(four servings)

Crisp sweet apple slices, rich toasted pecans, big chewy raisins, and tender small-leafed spinach come together with a bold chutney dressing.

1 cup pecan halves
2 bunches (about 1½ pounds) young, small-leaf spinach

2 Red Delicious apples
½ cup muscat raisins
½ cup chopped scallions

Chutney Dressing
½ cup vegetable oil
4 tablespoons mango-ginger chutney (I prefer Sharwood Mango-ginger)

1 teaspoon curry powder
1 teaspoon dry mustard
½ teaspoon salt
2 tablespoons lemon juice

Preheat the oven to 300°F.

Spread the pecans out on a baking sheet and toast for about 12 minutes (watch carefully so they don't burn). Meanwhile, wash, stem, and dry the spinach. Then, leaving the apples unpeeled, core, halve, and cut them crosswise into thin slices.

Put the spinach, apples, pecans, raisins, and scallions in a large salad bowl and toss to mix.

Put the oil, chutney, curry powder, dry mustard, salt, and lemon juice in a bowl, and stir until well mixed. Add the dressing to the salad and toss gently to coat all the ingredients. Serve immediately.

Green Rose Salad

(four servings)

Crisp lettuce leaves in a roselike shape are filled with colorful vegetables and served in one large bowl with thick buttermilk or ranch dressing passed on the side. This idea came from Myrtle Allen, one of the owners of Ballymaloe, a lovely inn and cooking school in County Cork, Ireland.

Buttermilk Dressing
½ cup buttermilk
½ cup mayonnaise
2 teaspoons finely chopped
    garlic (or put through a garlic
    press)

½ teaspoon salt

½ pound fresh beets; or 1 cup
    canned sliced beets, plain or
    pickled
1 head iceberg lettuce
1 bunch watercress
2 tomatoes

1 cucumber
1 bunch scallions
4 hard-boiled eggs, shelled and
    quartered (see page 187)
¾ cup large pitted black olives

To make the buttermilk dressing, put the buttermilk, mayonnaise, garlic, and salt in a jar with a lid and shake until well blended. Refrigerate until needed.

If using fresh beets, cut off all but an inch of the beet tops; don't pare or remove the roots. Drop the beets into enough boiling water to cover them and cook them, uncovered, until they are tender, 30 minutes to an hour, depending on their size. Drain the beets, drop them in cold water to cool them, slip off their skins, and slice.

To prepare the lettuce, fill a large bowl with cold water, core the lettuce, and forcefully plunge it, cored end down, into the water. Shake free of excess water and wrap the head in several layers of towel. Refrigerate for at least 6 hours or overnight before using. (This process not only ensures ultimate crispness, it separates the leaves and makes them easier to peel away without tearing.) Carefully separate the lettuce leaves. Remove the tough stems from the watercress, then wash and dry. Cut the tomatoes into wedges. Peel, seed, and slice the cucumber. Slice the scallions.

Arrange the lettuce leaves like a rose in a large bowl, with the large leaves on the outside and the smaller ones in the center. Put sprigs of watercress, the tomato wedges, and the beet and cucumber slices and scallions between the leaves. Tuck the egg quarters and olives around the top. Pass the dressing at the table.

Asparagus Salad

(four servings)

It's a cheery sight to see the first bundles of asparagus in the super-markets. Asparagus is always a treat served simply with melted butter, salt, and pepper, but since most of us can't leave well enough alone, I am including one of my favorite vinaigrette dressings for chilled, lightly cooked asparagus. The sesame seed oil gives this dressing a toasted nutty flavor. Serve with Deviled Eggs (see page 186).

2 pounds fresh asparagus	1 head butter lettuce
Dressing	
2 tablespoons white wine	1 tablespoon finely chopped
vinegar	parsley
1½ teaspoons Dijon mustard	6 tablespoons vegetable oil
¼ teaspoon salt	¼ to ½ teaspoon sesame seed
Pepper to taste	oil
1 tablespoon finely chopped	
scallion	

Wash the asparagus and cut or break off the tough colorless woody bottom of each stalk. If the asparagus spears are very large, peel a little of the coarse outer stalk at the butt end with a vegetable peeler. Plunge the spears into a large pot of boiling water and boil gently until they are just tender when pierced with a knife; begin testing after 5 minutes. When done, remove the spears and drain them. Put them on a plate, cover, and chill.

Separate enough lettuce leaves to make a bed for the asparagus. Wash and dry them, put in a plastic bag, and chill.

Mix together the vinegar, mustard, salt, pepper, scallion, and parsley in a bowl. Slowly add the vegetable oil and whisk until blended. Add the sesame seed oil, beginning with ¼ teaspoon, then taste. Just a faint nutty flavor should be present—add a little more if necessary but don't overdo. Cover and refrigerate.

When ready to serve, make a bed of butter lettuce leaves on a serving platter or on individual plates and arrange the asparagus spears on top. Spoon the vinaigrette over and serve cold.

Potato Salad

(four servings)

Potato salad makes a wonderful supper served with lots of whole hard-cooked eggs and a platter of lettuce and tomatoes. The secret to making this good potato salad is to toss the potatoes while they are still hot with the lemon juice and oil.

2 pounds red or white potatoes	3 stalks celery, diced
¼ cup olive oil	About 1¼ cups mayonnaise
¼ cup lemon juice	Salt and pepper to taste

Boil the potatoes until barely tender, about 15 minutes (potatoes continue to cook after they have been removed from the heat). Drain, and, as soon as they are cool enough to handle, peel and cut into ½-inch cubes.

While the potatoes are still hot, put them into a mixing bowl, sprinkle with the oil and lemon juice, and toss until the cubes are completely coated. Add the celery and mayonnaise. Season with salt and pepper and toss until well distributed. Serve chilled or at room temperature.

NOTE: This salad needs enough salt, pepper, and lemon juice to give good balance. Be generous enough with the mayonnaise so the salad is moist.

Waldorf Salad

(six servings)

Waldorf Salad harkens back to the tearoom, where it was served with tiny crustless white chicken sandwiches. This recipe is quite generous with walnuts and celery, and the addition of applesauce makes a superior dressing.

Dressing

½ cup mayonnaise

½ cup applesauce

3 tablespoons honey

1 tablespoon lemon juice

3 or 4 crisp, firm, green apples
  (pippins or Granny Smiths)

2 or 3 stalks celery

1½ cups walnuts, in large
  pieces

Salt to taste

Butter or iceberg lettuce
  leaves, washed and dried

In a small bowl, mix together the mayonnaise, applesauce, honey, and lemon.

Leave the apples unpeeled, core, and cut into bite-size chunks. Chop the celery into ½-inch chunks. Put the apples, celery, and walnuts in a large bowl and sprinkle lightly with salt. Pour the dressing over, mix well, and serve on a bed of lettuce leaves.

Avocado and Bacon Salad

(four servings)

Opposites do attract, and when salty, crunchy bacon meets soft, creamy avocado, they live happily ever after.

Dressing

1½ teaspoons lemon juice
¼ cup sour cream

½ cup mayonnaise

8 slices bacon (about ½ pound)
⅓ cup finely chopped scallions
2 avocados, peeled and cubed

1 head iceberg lettuce, cored, rinsed, wrapped, and chilled (see page 11), cut into bite-size pieces
Salt and pepper to taste

To make the dressing, mix together the lemon juice, sour cream, and mayonnaise in a small bowl. Stir until smooth, and set aside.

Dice the bacon, fry until crisp, and pat dry with paper towels. Toss together the bacon, scallions, avocado, and lettuce in a large bowl, and season with salt and pepper. Add enough dressing to coat all the ingredients and toss gently.

Salmon Salad Niçoise

(four servings)

If you can't afford a trip to the south of France, a Niçoise salad is the next best thing. This variation uses salmon instead of the classic tuna fish. Make it when you have some leftover cooked salmon.

Vinaigrette

¼ cup white cider vinegar, or to taste

1 teaspoon salt, or to taste

½ teaspoon pepper

1 cup olive oil

2 tablespoons cold water*

10 small new potatoes

⅓ pound string beans (about 1½ cups)

3 ripe but firm tomatoes

1 green bell pepper

1 onion

Crisp lettuce leaves

About 1 pound cooked salmon (see page 60), flaked (approximately 2 cups)

½ cup Niçoise olives if available; or other black olives

About ¼ cup anchovies, cut in half lengthwise

2 tablespoons capers

1 lemon, cut into wedges, for garnish

To make the vinaigrette, mix together the vinegar and salt in a small bowl and let stand a few minutes. Add the pepper and slowly stir or whisk in the olive oil. Taste for acidity and salt, and add more vinegar and/or salt if too bland. Stir in the water, mixing

---

*The water in this vinaigrette helps emulsify the oil and vinegar, and it also reduces the cloying oiliness.

briskly. Stir to blend before using, or store in a jar with a tight and shake well before using.

Put the potatoes in a saucepan, cover with cold water, bring to a boil, and gently boil until tender when pierced with a knife, about 15 minutes. Drain, peel while hot but cool enough to handle, and cut into bite-size pieces. Wash the beans, remove the ends and strings, and cut into 1-inch pieces. Drop them into a large pot of boiling water and boil gently for 5 to 10 minutes (taste one to see if they are done—they should still be slightly crunchy). Drain the beans and rinse them thoroughly in cold water to stop the cooking.

Cut the tomatoes into wedges. Remove the seeds and veins from the pepper and cut it into thin slices. Cut the onion into thin rings and put in a bowl with ice water and ice cubes to keep crisp.

This salad may be arranged on one large platter or presented on large individual salad plates. Arrange the lettuce leaves to make a bed for the other ingredients. Put a mound of the salmon in the center and arrange the potatoes, beans, tomatoes, and olives in mounds around it. Put the anchovy strips, pepper slices, and onion rings on top. Sprinkle the capers over all. Just before serving, pour the vinaigrette over all, and put the lemon wedges around the plate.

You can toss the salad, but the presentation isn't as enticing.

Tuscan Bean and Tuna Salad

(four servings)

The Italians are masters at using tuna in inventive ways. Vitello tonnato (veal with a creamy tuna sauce) is one example, and this recipe is another.

1½ cups dried cannellini beans
  (or any other white beans);
  or 6 cups canned beans
  (be sure to rinse them with water
  and drain them before using)
Salt and coarsely ground
  pepper to taste
2 tablespoons red wine vinegar

6 tablespoons olive oil
1 tablespoon chopped fresh
  basil
½ cup chopped Italian parsley;
  plus sprigs for garnish
1 large onion, finely chopped
1 pound cooked tuna, flaked;
  or canned tuna

If using dried beans, rinse, pick through (discard any shriveled beans or foreign matter), put in a pot, cover with water, and allow to soak overnight; or try the short method—cover the beans with water, bring to a boil, cook for 1 minute, and then cover the pot and let stand for 1 hour. Drain the water from the beans. Put the beans in a large heavy-bottomed pot. Add enough water to cover the beans. Add ¾ teaspoon salt (½ teaspoon salt for every cup of dried beans). Bring to a boil over medium heat. Reduce the heat to a simmer, cover, and simmer about 1 hour, or until the beans are tender. Make sure the beans are covered with water while they're cooking.

When the beans are tender, drain them (if using canned beans, drain). Allow the beans to cool, and put them in a large serving bowl. Season with salt and pepper. In a small bowl stir together the vinegar and olive oil. Pour over the beans, and toss until well mixed. Sprinkle the basil and Italian parsley over the beans and toss again. Add the onion and tuna and mix. Garnish with the sprigs of Italian parsley.

Mustard Ring Salad

(six servings)

It seems that aspic and gelatin salads have completely fallen out of fashion, but I don't know of another salad that's better at showing off the flavors of seafood. This one is bright yellow like a sunflower, and it has a snappy, sharp turmeric and mustard taste. You will want to make the ring early in the day or even the night before, because it must be chilled at least four hours before serving.

1 envelope unflavored gelatin	½ teaspoon salt
1¼ cups cold water	1 teaspoon turmeric
4 eggs, well beaten	1 cup heavy cream, whipped
½ cup white vinegar	1½ pounds raw unshelled
½ cup sugar	shrimp
1½ tablespoons dry mustard	

Soak the gelatin in ¼ cup cold water for 5 minutes. Put the beaten eggs, cup of water, and white vinegar in a heavy-bottomed saucepan or the top of a double boiler, and stir to blend. Add the gelatin, sugar, mustard, salt, and turmeric, and mix well. Heat the mixture over medium-low heat, stirring constantly, for about 5 minutes. Do not allow the mixture to boil. Remove from the heat and cool. Gently stir in the whipped cream. Pour into a 1½-quart ring mold and chill for 4 to 5 hours before serving.

Bring a large pot of salted water to a boil and add the raw shrimp. Turn the heat down so the water is boiling gently and cook the shrimp until they turn pink, about 1 to 3 minutes. Drain. When cool enough to handle, shell and devein the shrimp. Mound the shrimp in the middle of the mustard ring and serve.

Buffalo Chicken Wing Salad

(four servings)

Not buffalo as in the beast, but Buffalo as in western New York State, where spicy chicken wings with blue cheese dressing originated. Adding the cold crunch of celery and iceberg lettuce to the heat of the pepper and the bite of blue cheese makes an even greater combination of tastes and textures than Buffalo chicken wings alone. Individuals vary in their tolerance for heat, but this salad needs fire to succeed; those who want their Buffalo wings hotter yet can pass a bottle of Louisiana hot sauce at the table.

Blue Cheese Dressing

1 cup mayonnaise

2 tablespoons grated onion

1 teaspoon finely chopped garlic

1 tablespoon lemon juice

1 tablespoon white vinegar

Salt and pepper to taste

Optional: cayenne pepper

¼ cup crumbled blue cheese

⅓ cup flour

1 teaspoon salt, or to taste

2 teaspoons cayenne pepper, or to taste

1 to 1½ pounds chicken drumettes (12 to 16 chicken wings, second joints and wing tips removed)

3 tablespoons vegetable oil

1 head iceberg lettuce, cored, rinsed, wrapped, and chilled (see page 11), cut into bite-size pieces

4 to 5 stalks celery, cut into 2- by ¼-inch strips

To make the dressing, mix together the mayonnaise, onion, garlic, lemon juice, and vinegar, and blend until smooth. Taste and correct the seasoning, adding salt, pepper, and optional cayenne as desired. Gently stir in the blue cheese.

Put the flour, salt, and cayenne in a bag and shake until mixed. Add the chicken to the bag and shake until all the pieces are well coated with the flour mixture.

Heat the oil in a large skillet, put in the chicken, and fry over a medium-high heat, turning the pieces occasionally, until all are cooked through, about 12 to 15 minutes. Remove from the heat and shake more cayenne and salt over the wings; don't be timid— this makes the dish lively. Set aside.

Put the lettuce and celery in a large salad bowl. Pour the dressing over and toss until the lettuce is evenly coated. Arrange the chicken pieces on top of the lettuce around the edges of the bowl. Serve at once.

"Avoid having too many courses. If the food is good, that is all the more reason to limit the number of dishes, so that each may be fully savored . . .

"Give as much care to simple dishes and the humbler foods as you do to elaborate dishes and ambitious menus. At the same time, do not neglect to take advantage of new developments in the growing, shipping, preserving, and cooking of food. Take time both to cherish the old and to investigate the new."

—from *The Fireside Cookbook*
by James Beard

Beef Salad with Sour Pickles

(six servings)

I would always prefer having leftover roast beef cold in a salad like this rather than eating it reheated.

3 hard-boiled eggs (see page 187)

3 cups thinly sliced, bite-size pieces cooked roast beef

4 medium potatoes, boiled, peeled, and sliced

1 bunch scallions, sliced

4 to 5 stalks celery, coarsely chopped

1½ cups large bite-size chunks of dill pickles

Dressing

1 tablespoon Dijon mustard

¾ cup olive oil

1 clove garlic, finely chopped and mashed with ¾ teaspoon salt

½ teaspoon freshly ground pepper

2 tablespoons red wine vinegar

2 tablespoons cold water*

¼ teaspoon Tabasco, or to taste

Optional: ¼ cup capers

Shell the hard-boiled eggs and separate the yolks from the whites. Set aside the yolks. Dice the whites and mix together in a large salad bowl with the beef, potatoes, scallions, celery, and pickles.

To make the dressing, in a small bowl mash the reserved egg yolks with a fork and stir in the mustard, olive oil, the garlic and salt, pepper, vinegar, water, and Tabasco. Taste the dressing and adjust the seasonings if necessary.

Pour the dressing over the beef salad and toss. Pass around the capers in a small bowl at the table, if you wish.

*The water in this dressing helps emulsify the oil and vinegar, and it also reduces the cloying oiliness.

Supper Soups

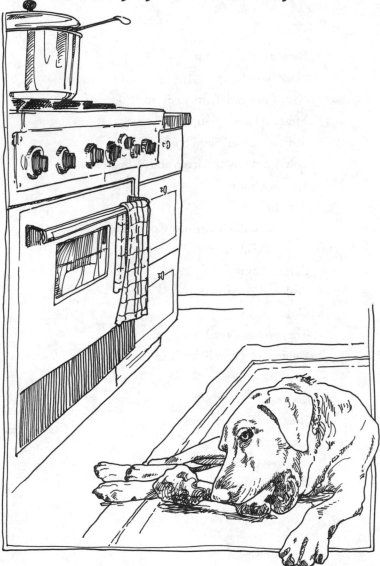

Ham and Bean Soup

Black Bean Soup

Navy Bean and Tomato Soup

Mustard Green Soup

Sharon's Lentil Salsa Soup

Celery Soup with Green and White Beans

Split Pea Soup

Borscht

Joyce McGillis's Creamy Corn Soup

Posole Salad Soup

Eggplant Soup

Leek and Potato Soup

Onion Soup

Tomato and Bread Soup

Chinese Hot and Sour Soup

Fish Chowder

Cioppino

Cream of Scallop Soup

Oyster Stew

Chicken Custard in Broth

Rich Chicken Noodle Soup

When I was very young the virtues of soup eluded me. I always wanted to start right in with the good solid dishes, and soup seemed superfluous. I lived a long time before I truly appreciated the soothing, satisfying qualities of a bowl of soup. But into every home cook's life there comes a moment when it's time to make soup.

When I was first married, my husband had several favorite dishes that his mother used to make, and one of them was a ham and bean soup. I tried to re-create the soup of his memory with one recipe after another. I added sage to ham and beans, I added thyme, I added everything but the kitchen sink. And each time he tasted my latest effort he would shake his head—nothing came close. This went on for almost two years. (To this day I don't know why I didn't contact my mother-in-law, Cecilia, right away. I guess I thought the next soup was going to be *it*.) When I finally asked for the recipe and Cecilia sent it to me, I was flabbergasted. It only took four plain and simple ingredients: beans, onions, ham, and water. It was a basic cooking lesson I have never forgotten: less can be more.

Soup runs the gamut from fancy clarified soups with expensive garnishes to peasant soups of bread and water. The soups in this chapter are not the light kind that tease the appetite; they are intended to fortify. They are solid and nourishing and meant to be the main event at suppertime. And they demonstrate all the virtues of soup: convenience, simplicity, frugality, and wholesomeness.

Soup making is often misunderstood. I used to be amazed that the students in my cooking classes thought that making soup was necessarily a long and arduous process of watching and stirring. You do not have to be an all-day babysitter to a simmering soup pot. Nor should soup be a catchall or a way of getting rid of tired vegetables. I'm leery of cooks who advise you to clear out the vegetable bins of your refrigerator and add the contents to the soup pot. Soup should be thought out and made with care. Once you've made it, it's a meal you can take out of the refrigerator and have ready in a hurry. And it's the one dish most easily extended for the unexpected guest.

Good soup depends on critical tasting and seasoning. Nothing is less appealing than a bland soup. Don't be timid about seasoning. It may surprise you to discover how much salt is needed to bring out the good flavor of a soup. The trick is to add carefully, and stir and taste after each addition. Always add only a little salt at the beginning, remembering that simmering causes evaporation and salt concentration; the final critical correction should take place just before serving.

If you have a neglected soup tureen that you inherited or got for a wedding present, get it down off the shelf where it's gathering dust and use it! There is nothing more welcoming than soup being ladled from a big steaming tureen at suppertime.

Ham and Bean Soup

(four servings)

Ham and Bean Soup holds a special place in my heart because it was one of my first and best lessons in cooking: making it fancy won't make it better.

1 pound (about 2 cups) Great Northern beans, soaked overnight and drained (see page 18)	2 onions, chopped 2 cups cut-up ham or smoked pork butt Salt and pepper to taste

Put the beans, onions, and ham pieces in a large pot. Pour in enough cold water to cover the beans by 1½ inches. Bring the mixture to a boil over medium heat. Reduce the heat to a simmer, removing any scum that rises to the surface. Simmer about 2 hours, or until the beans are tender. Add water, if needed.

Season with salt and pepper. Skim off any fat that rises to the top and serve.

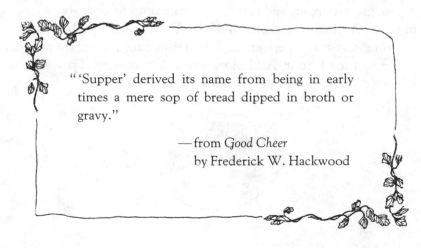

"'Supper' derived its name from being in early times a mere sop of bread dipped in broth or gravy."

—from *Good Cheer*
by Frederick W. Hackwood

Black Bean Soup

(six servings)

Black beans have a rich flavor and their dramatic color looks striking with white rice or sour cream, purple onion, lemon slices,
chopped chiles, and hard-boiled egg. In the Caribbean, black beans
are served with white rice in a dish called Moors and Christians.

1 pound (about 2 cups) dried black beans, soaked overnight (see page 18)	1 large green bell pepper, peeled, seeded, and chopped
About 2½ teaspoons salt	6 cloves garlic, chopped
½ cup olive oil	1¼ teaspoons dried oregano
1 large onion, chopped	¼ teaspoon cayenne pepper
	½ teaspoon black pepper

Drain the beans, and put them in a large pot. Add enough water to
cover the beans by 1½ inches and 1 teaspoon salt and cook over
medium heat for 45 minutes.

Heat the olive oil in a large heavy-bottomed skillet, add the
onion, green pepper, and garlic, and sauté until tender, about 2 or 3
minutes. Add the vegetables to the beans and then add the oregano,
cayenne, and black pepper, and the remaining 1½ teaspoons salt.

Simmer for 1 hour. Add more water, if necessary. Taste for seasoning, and add more salt if needed.

Navy Bean and Tomato Soup

(four servings)

One more of those lessons in cooking that teaches you how a mea-
ger list of ingredients doesn't necessarily result in a meager-tasting
soup. All it takes here is a sure hand with seasoning, but with the
salt pork, watch your addition of salt.

½ pound (about 1 cup) dried
   white navy beans, soaked
   overnight (see page 18)
28-ounce can whole tomatoes
2 onions, chopped
½ pound salt pork, cut into
   small pieces

2 cloves garlic, finely chopped
1 teaspoon dried thyme
Salt and pepper to taste
About 4 cups water

Drain the water from the beans and put them in a large heavy-bottomed pot. Stir in the tomatoes, onions, salt pork, garlic, thyme,
and salt and pepper and add the water, making sure it covers the
contents of the pot. Simmer for 3½ hours, or until the beans are
tender. Adjust the seasonings and serve.

Mustard Green Soup

(four servings)

I wish people would get braver about using mustard greens. They are in almost every supermarket now. I remember driving around with my Italian mother and grandmother many years ago and stopping by yellow fields to gather wild mustard greens, which were then cooked with garlic and dressed with olive oil and vinegar. Navy beans have an unobtrusive flavor that blends well with the bite of bitter greens. Serve with wheat rolls and a mild cheese like fontina.

2 pounds turnips, peeled and diced
4 tablespoons olive oil
About 3 cloves garlic, finely chopped
1 large leek (or 1 large onion), chopped
2 cups cooked navy beans (see page 18)

½ pound mustard greens (or any bitter greens), washed and coarsely chopped
6 cups chicken broth (see page 47)
Salt and pepper to taste

In a pot of boiling water, cook the turnips for about 5 minutes. Drain and reserve.

Heat the olive oil in a soup kettle or pot. Add the garlic and leek and cook over medium-low heat, stirring often, until the garlic and leek are softened but not browned. Stir in the turnip, beans, greens, and broth. Add salt and pepper to taste, and simmer for about 15 minutes. Serve hot.

Sharon's Lentil Salsa Soup

(four to six servings)

I never knew that lentils were used in Mexican cooking until I tried this recipe. The peppy salsa adds flavor to the earthy lentils. (By the way, some people seem to think you need to presoak lentils before you cook them. You don't.)

1 tablespoon olive oil	1¼ cups lentils
3 cloves garlic, finely chopped	2 cups Red Salsa (see page
2 carrots, peeled and sliced	164)
1 onion, chopped	1½ teaspoons salt
6 cups water	

Put the olive oil in a soup pot (I use a 6-quart pot) and spread it so it films the bottom. Set over medium heat and stir in the garlic, carrots, and onion. Cook, stirring constantly, until the vegetables are softened, but not brown. Add the water, lentils, Red Salsa, and salt. Cover, let the soup come to a boil, then reduce the heat so that it bubbles without boiling too hard. Occasionally stir and check that the water isn't boiling away, adding a little water if the soup gets too thick. Simmer for about 45 minutes, or until the lentils are tender. Serve hot.

Supper Alone

Sometimes eating supper alone feels private, quiet, and blessedly liberating. You may eat anything you want; you needn't be conventional. I like a baked potato with olive oil and coarse salt and pepper followed by vanilla ice cream, which proves to me that money doesn't buy a good meal. One night not long ago I had freshly baked cookies and milk, and found that uplifting.

If my spirit is less than cheerful, it helps me to fix something restorative when eating alone. Split Pea Soup (see page 34) is easy to make—it takes only a few minutes to get started and is ready in 1 to 1½ hours. Kitchen preparations, the busyness of chopping, stirring, and watching a bubbling pot, can help dispel any gloom, at least for me.

I like to fix supper on a tray and carry it back to the desk in my bedroom. I have a fireplace there and I can sit and eat while listening to music or watching the news on TV. Eating in bed will always seem like the height of luxury to me, but spilling one's soup on the bed destroys the mood, so only food that doesn't slosh is recommended.

Celery Soup with Green and White Beans

(six servings)

Celery has a delicate flavor and is a faint presence in many soups, but here it gets to stand up on its own. The beans add texture, color, and body.

About 8 stalks celery, coarsely chopped	1½ cups cooked Great Northern beans (see page 18)
1 large onion, diced	10 ounces (2 cups) frozen lima beans
4 cups chicken broth (see page 47)	Salt and pepper to taste

Put the celery and onion in a large pot, add 3 cups of the chicken broth, and bring to a boil. Reduce the heat and simmer for 15 minutes, or until the vegetables are tender.

Drain and reserve the liquid from the vegetables. Put the vegetables in a food processor or blender, adding a little of the hot liquid, and process until puréed. Put the puréed vegetables back in the pot with the hot liquid and the rest of the chicken stock. Add the beans and simmer for 10 minutes, or until the beans are heated through. Salt and pepper to taste, being careful not to add too much pepper—a little goes a long way.

Split Pea Soup

(four servings)

Many old-fashioned pea soups were stodgy. Today's split pea soups are a brighter color and have a far fresher flavor. These days you don't have to presoak the peas, so you can count on an hour to an hour and a half to put Split Pea Soup on your table. Serve with dark rye bread and melon.

1 pound (2 cups) split green peas
1½ pounds ham hocks, or a
   leftover ham bone with a little
   meat attached
2 medium onions, chopped

3 stalks celery with leaves,
   chopped
8 cups water
Salt and pepper to taste

Put the split peas, ham hocks, onions, and celery in a soup pot, add the water, and bring to a boil. Reduce the heat to medium, and lightly salt and pepper. Cook, stirring occasionally, for 1 to 1½ hours. The soup is done when the peas are soft. Taste, add more salt, if needed, and a generous amount of pepper. Remove the bones and any skin from the ham hocks, and shred the meat if the chunks are too large.

If a smooth soup is desired, remove the meat and purée the soup. I don't bother, and rather like the slight texture that the peas have when they are whole.

Borscht

(six servings)

This borscht is so chunky and thick that it's almost not a soup at all. If you want it more soupy, just add two to three more cups of broth. Borscht has a nice taste of beet sweetness and lemon sourness.

4 medium potatoes, peeled
1 large onion
2 carrots
4 to 5 stalks celery
2 tablespoons chopped fresh parsley
6 cups beef broth
2 pounds fresh beets, peeled and finely chopped

1½ tablespoons lemon juice
2 tablespoons fresh chopped dill; plus a little more for garnish, if desired
2 tablespoons sugar
Salt to taste
Optional: ½ cup sour cream, for garnish

Finely chop the potatoes, onion, carrots, and celery, either by hand or in a food processor. Put the vegetables, parsley, and beef broth in an 8-quart heavy-bottomed pot. Bring to a boil over medium heat. Reduce the heat and simmer for 30 minutes. Add the beets, and simmer for another 30 minutes. Remove from the heat and add the lemon juice, dill, sugar, and salt. If you like, serve garnished with a little more chopped dill, and pass around the sour cream in a small bowl.

Joyce McGillis's
Creamy Corn Soup

(four servings)

It takes only three ingredients to make creamy corn soup. Serve with a grilled cheese and tomato sandwich or, if you're lazy, with Rye Crackers (see page 145).

6 cups corn kernels—fresh (about 9 ears), frozen, or canned and drained	4½ cups milk ½ teaspoon salt, or to taste

If you are using fresh corn, first cut the kernels from the cob with a sharp knife. Put the corn, 3 cups of the milk, and salt in a heavy-bottomed saucepan and bring to a boil. Reduce the heat and simmer for 20 minutes.

Pour the milk and corn mixture into a food processor and process until the corn is puréed. Add the remaining 1½ cups milk and process until well blended. Correct salt if necessary. Return to the saucepan and gently reheat, stirring frequently.

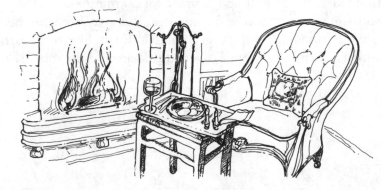

Posole Salad Soup

(six servings)

It may seem weird putting your salad in the middle of your soup. It isn't. The salad looks great and stays crunchy in the middle of the soup, adding a sparkling contrast in texture. Posole is the Spanish name for hominy soup.

4 cups chicken broth (see page 47)

2 teaspoons ground cumin

2 cups canned stewed tomatoes, broken up

6 tablespoons masa harina* in 1 cup cold water, blended until smooth

Salt and pepper to taste

3 cups canned yellow or white hominy,† drained

1 cup coarsely chopped cilantro

2 cups coarsely chopped iceberg lettuce

1 avocado, peeled, pitted, and cut into 1-inch dice

In a large saucepan, stir together the broth, cumin, tomatoes, masa harina mixture, salt and pepper, and hominy. Bring to a boil, reduce the heat, and simmer for 5 minutes, stirring occasionally. Toss together the cilantro and lettuce in a bowl. Add the avocado to the soup just before serving. Serve the soup, and pass around the lettuce and cilantro at the table, letting everyone put some on top of their soup.

*Masa harina is corn treated with lime water and ground into a flour. With the addition of water it makes the dough used for tamales and tortillas. Quaker Oats makes masa harina that is widely available in supermarkets.
†Hominy is dried corn that has had its hull and germ removed with lye or soda.

Eggplant Soup

(four servings)

There's no middle ground on the issue of eggplants: either you're an eggplant lover or an eggplant loather. This recipe will satisfy eggplant lovers, because it's thick, creamy, and all eggplant. Serve with Garlic Rolls (see page 149) and a tomato salad.

2 eggplants, about 1 pound each	Salt and pepper to taste
Olive oil	4 cups chicken broth (see page 47)

Preheat the oven to 375°F.

Remove the stems from the eggplants and cut them into ½-inch lengthwise slices. Brush both sides of the slices with olive oil, salt and pepper them, and place on baking sheets in a single layer. Bake for 20 to 25 minutes, until lightly golden and completely tender when pierced with a fork. Using a spoon, remove the pulp from the skin.

Put the pulp and 2 cups of the broth into a food processor and process until smooth. (If you don't have a food processor, pass the pulp through a food mill.) Pour into a saucepan, stir in the remaining broth, and gently heat until hot. Taste for salt and pepper. Add more broth for a thinner soup.

Leek and Potato Soup

(four servings)

Whenever I see leek and potato soup on a restaurant menu or in a cookbook, I've come to expect a purée rich with heavy cream. *This* soup is neither puréed nor enriched, so it has more character and a homey texture. Bread, fruit, and Almond Diamond cookies (see page 210) complete the supper.

1½ tablespoons butter	3 medium potatoes, peeled
3 leeks, washed thoroughly	and diced
and thinly sliced	2¾ cups milk
2 stalks celery, thinly sliced	Salt and pepper to taste
1½ cups water	

Melt the butter in a large heavy-bottomed pot. Put in the leeks and celery and cook over moderate heat for 10 minutes, stirring often to prevent sticking. Stir in 1 cup of the water, cover, and cook for 10 more minutes. Add the potatoes and the remaining ½ cup of water, stir, cover, and cook over low heat for 10 more minutes. Stir in the milk, cover, and cook 10 minutes, or until the potatoes are tender. Add salt and pepper to taste, and serve.

Onion Soup

(four servings)

For economy, this is the next best thing to stone soup. It takes just two pounds of onions to feed four people. But there is one thing you cannot skimp on when you're making onion soup, and that's the time it takes to caramelize the onions. You have to cook them slowly for about an hour until they've turned a rich golden brown. That's where all the flavor comes from.

2 tablespoons vegetable oil	4 slices completely dried
7 large onions, thinly sliced	French-style bread
Salt to taste	2 ounces Monterey Jack
6 cups water	cheese, grated (⅔ cup)

Put the oil in a large heavy-bottomed skillet. Add the onions, lightly salt, and cook patiently over medium-low heat for 1 hour, stirring every 5 to 10 minutes.

After 1 hour, when the onions have caramelized and turned a rich golden brown, add the water, cover, and simmer for 30 minutes. Put a slice of the bread in each bowl, sprinkle about 2 tablespoons of cheese over each bread slice, and ladle the onion soup over the bread. Serve hot.

Tomato and Bread Soup

(four servings)

How can anything as humble and insignificant as stale bread be transformed into something so absolutely good as this soup?

⅔ cup olive oil
4 cloves garlic, crushed
2 large onions, finely chopped
6 medium tomatoes, peeled, seeded, and chopped
4 cups chicken broth (see page 47)

½ loaf French bread, sliced and broken into pieces
3 ounces Parmesan cheese, freshly grated (1 cup)

Heat the oil in a large heavy-bottomed saucepan over medium heat. Stir in the garlic and onions and cook until soft, about 1 to 2 minutes. Add the tomatoes and simmer for 10 minutes—watch carefully and stir often. Pour in the broth, stir to blend, and bring to a boil. While the soup is boiling, add the bread pieces, and continue to cook over medium heat for 2 more minutes. Cover and let stand for 1 hour, then reheat and serve. (This may be served without reheating, but the flavors are stronger when the soup is allowed to stand.) Pass around a bowl of the grated Parmesan cheese at the table.

Chinese Hot and Sour Soup

(eight cups or four servings)

Here is a light and spicy recipe everyone will ask for after they've tasted it. Serve with warm flour tortillas spread with plum sauce (available in Chinese markets or in the international sections of supermarkets) and sprinkled with scallions, and have The Best Rice Pudding (see page 217) for dessert.

6 cups chicken broth (see page 47)

¼ pound fresh mushrooms, wiped clean and sliced (1½ cups)

¼ pound fresh raw spinach, washed (1½ cups)

3 tablespoons light soy sauce

3 tablespoons cider vinegar

¾ teaspoon black pepper

2¼ tablespoons sesame seed oil

½ teaspoon hot pepper oil or Tabasco sauce (taste the soup carefully before adding the full amount)

¾ pound tofu (soybean cake, found in the produce section of most supermarkets), cut into small dice

3 tablespoons cornstarch, dissolved in 5 tablespoons water

1 egg, beaten

3 tablespoons finely chopped cilantro

2 scallions, finely chopped

Put the chicken broth, mushrooms, and spinach in a soup pot. Simmer for 4 minutes.

Mix the soy sauce, vinegar, pepper, sesame seed oil, and the hot pepper oil or Tabasco together in a small bowl. Stir until well blended and then add to the broth. Taste and correct the seasonings.

Add the tofu and the cornstarch, stirring constantly until the soup thickens. Pour the beaten egg into the simmering broth, and continue to stir until the egg forms ribbons. Add the cilantro and scallions and serve at once.

Fish Chowder

(four servings)

I have tasted New England chowders and Manhattan chowders, and New England chowder wins my vote. A whole small new potato in the middle of the bowl is a friendly touch.

4 new potatoes, peeled and left whole (potatoes must be hot when served)	4 cups milk
	Salt and pepper to taste
1½ pounds firm-fleshed white fish fillets	1 tablespoon fresh thyme plus 1 tablespoon dried thyme; or 1½ tablespoons dried thyme
¼ cup diced salt pork	
1 onion, chopped	½ cup chopped parsley
3 medium potatoes, peeled and thinly sliced (about ⅛ inch thick)	

Put the 4 new potatoes in a medium-size pot and boil in salted water for about 20 minutes, then cover to keep warm and set aside. While the potatoes are cooking, cut the fish into chunks, put it in another pot with 2 cups water, and simmer for 3 or 4 minutes over medium heat. Remove from the heat and set aside.

In a large soup pot cook the salt pork until it is golden brown; with a slotted spoon scoop up the browned pork, drain on paper towels, and set aside; discard all but 2 tablespoons of the pork fat left in the pot. Add the onion and cook until softened, about 2 to 3 minutes. Drain the fish cooking liquid into the pot, reserving the fish; add the 3 sliced potatoes, and more water, if needed, to cover. Boil until the potatoes are cooked, about 10 minutes. Add the fish, milk, salt and pepper, and the thyme. Just heat thoroughly, don't boil.

Put one of the whole, cooked potatoes in the center of each soup bowl, ladle in the soup, and sprinkle around a few of the fried pork bits. Scatter the parsley over all, and serve.

Cioppino

(six servings)

There are about as many versions of cioppino, the Italian fish stew, as there are cooks who make it. You can be creative here and use whatever fish or shellfish you like. There are no rigid rules, but have a good loaf of Italian sourdough bread with this.

¼ cup olive oil	1 teaspoon dried oregano
3 cloves garlic, minced	1 teaspoon sugar
2 pounds fresh white fish fillets, cut into large chunks	2 bay leaves
	Salt and pepper to taste
1 cup dry white wine	1 cup chopped parsley
About 8 Italian plum tomatoes (1 pound), finely chopped	

Heat the oil in a large sauté pan over medium heat. Add the garlic and cook about 1 minute, until just softened, but not brown. Add ½ cup of the fish, then the wine, tomatoes, oregano, sugar, bay leaves, and salt and pepper. Bring to a simmer, cover, and cook for 5 minutes. Add the remaining fish and cook, covered, for about 5 minutes more. Sprinkle with the parsley and serve.

Cream of Scallop Soup

(four servings)

What's best about this soup is the flavors of fresh dill and briny scallops. Serve with Lemon Crackers (see page 146) and a big bowl of chopped seeded cucumbers mixed with scallions.

5 tablespoons butter	2 pounds scallops, cut into
2 tablespoons finely chopped	¼-inch pieces (4 cups)
onion	1½ tablespoons chopped
5 tablespoons flour	fresh dill; or 1 teaspoon
4 cups milk	dried dill
½ bay leaf	Salt and pepper to taste

Melt the butter in a soup pot over medium heat. Add the onion and cook for about 5 minutes, until it is soft and translucent. Stir in the flour and cook over low heat for 2 minutes. Stir in the milk, bay leaf, and 1 cup of the scallops, and simmer for 5 minutes.

Remove the bay leaf. Add the remaining scallops, 1 tablespoon of the fresh dill or all of the dried, and salt and pepper. Heat for 1 minute and serve. Sprinkle the rest of the fresh dill over the soup just before serving.

Oyster Stew

(four servings)

Everyone is crazy about oysters on the half shell these days, but hardly anyone remembers that oyster stew can be even better.

3 cups milk
2 cups heavy cream
2½ cups shucked fresh oysters
   with their liquor

Salt and pepper to taste
3 tablespoons butter

Heat the milk and cream in a pan, but do not boil. Add the oysters and their liquor and simmer just until the edges of the oysters curl a little, about 1 minute. Season with salt and pepper, and add the butter. Heat until the butter melts, and serve very hot.

Chicken Custard in Broth

(four servings)

Young children will love this. They can break up the custard into pieces and let it float about in the broth to look like small boats and shore birds.

1 cup chopped cooked chicken
   meat (approximately 1 whole
   chicken breast)
6⅓ cups chicken broth (recipe
   follows)

4 eggs
1½ ounces Parmesan cheese,
   freshly grated (½ cup)
Salt and pepper to taste

Preheat the oven to 350°F.

Butter 4 ramekin dishes, each about ½ cup in size (I use Pyrex). Put the chicken, ⅓ cup of the chicken broth, eggs, Parmesan cheese, and salt and pepper in a food processor or blender and process until smooth. Pour the mixture into the prepared ramekins and place them in a shallow baking dish or pan filled with enough boiling water to come up the sides of the ramekins by 1 inch.

Place the water bath in the oven and bake for 12 to 15 minutes, checking the custard after 10 minutes; when it is just firm around the edges and trembly in the center it is done. Be careful not to overcook. Meanwhile, heat the rest of the chicken broth. Remove the custards from the oven and invert each dish in a soup bowl. Surround the custards with hot chicken broth and serve.

Rich Chicken Noodle Soup

(six servings)

This chicken soup is the real thing. You make your own rich broth, strain it, and then turn it into a supper dish with egg noodles and chicken pieces. Serve it with dinner rolls, and have strawberry ice cream for dessert.

Chicken Broth
2½ pounds chicken backs, wings, necks
9 cups cold water
1 onion, cut in half
2 carrots, cut in thirds

3 stalks celery, with leaves, cut in half
1 bay leaf
1 teaspoon dried thyme, crumbled

Salt and pepper to taste
4 ounces flat dried egg noodles
½ chicken breast, skinned, boned, and cut into tiny pieces

1½ tablespoons finely chopped parsley

Put the chicken backs, wings, necks, the water, onion, carrots, celery, bay leaf, and thyme in a soup pot and bring to a boil. Reduce to a simmer and cook for 1 hour. Remove from the heat and strain the broth through two layers of paper towel into a bowl or large measuring cup. You will have approximately 6½ cups.

Add enough water to the broth to make 8 cups. Return the liquid to the soup pot, turn the heat to medium, and add salt and pepper and the egg noodles. Cook, simmering, for 10 minutes. Add the chicken breast pieces and simmer 5 minutes more. Remove from the heat, add the parsley, and cool. Refrigerate until needed. Reheat and serve hot.

Fish and Shellfish

Fillet of Sole with Fresh Bread Crumbs

Halibut Baked on Vegetables

Sweet Walnuts and Prawns

Laguna Beach Shrimp Curry

Baltimore Crab Cakes

Salmon with Cucumber and Caper Sauce

Scandinavian Salmon Sandwich

Tarragon Fish on Toast

Fish Tacos

Oyster Buns

Scallops with Corn and Cilantro

During the early 1940s, the war years, I was in Laguna Beach, California, learning to cook. My husband was in the Marine Corps, stationed nearby, and we had rented a tiny house close to the ocean. During the five years we lived there, every friend we knew from our school days arrived to visit (and often to stay). I loved those years—cooking and eating with cheery, hungry friends.

Among my great memories of that time are grunion hunts, which were wildly suspenseful and always exciting. Grunions are small silvery fish about five inches long that belong to the smelt family. They spawn during the summer on the beach above high tide, by the light of the full moon. Grunion runs are accurately predicted by the Fish and Game Department, but no one knows on which stretch of beach they will choose to spawn; it could be Santa Monica or San Juan Capistrano.

On the appointed night we would congregate on the main beach in Laguna at about ten o'clock, along with lots of other grunion enthusiasts. Groups of us spread out along the beach, sitting around fires, while the full moon made a path across the water. We would watch and wait while we talked about the last grunion run.

The popular alcoholic beverages in those days were Southern Comfort and beer, and they were in ample supply at all grunion runs. If we were lucky, and in the right spot, the magic moment would arrive around midnight and someone would yell, "Here they come!" The sight of those shining, silvery fish wiggling on the sand was most unbelievable. We would grab pails and head into the surf, facing the beach knee-deep in water, so we could catch the grunions as they were swept past us, back into the tides. They would be on the beach for only seconds, but for several hours wave after wave would bring in more.

Gazing down the beach when the grunions were running heavily, it looked as though bits of stars were strewn on the sand. We had to use our hands to catch the fish—it is illegal to use nets. It was almost dawn when we carried our buckets home. We would fix the grunions simply, frying them quickly in sizzling bacon fat, and serve them with scrambled eggs and buttered toast.

More than any other food you cook, fish has to be fresh. If it's not it loses all its better qualities. I've been spoiled by those early Laguna days of eating fish and shellfish as fresh as those grunions. When you shop for fish, be sure it has a clean, briny smell. I know I've annoyed supermarket clerks by returning fish fillets after I've opened the plastic wrap, but let's face it, if it smells fishy, it isn't fresh.

Fillet of Sole with Fresh Bread Crumbs

(four servings)

Pan-frying fish with bread crumbs is as good a way as any I know of fixing fish. Serve with the tiny creamy pasta called orzo (see Orzo with Fresh Dill, page 186). The orzo will be even better with fish if it has some grated lemon zest added to it.

1½ pounds fillets of sole, or other white fish	3 tablespoons butter
½ cup flour	⅓ cup dried coarse bread crumbs
Salt and pepper to taste	2 lemons, quartered
2 tablespoons olive oil	

If the fish fillets are very thin, make one fat fillet from two fillets by stacking one on top of the other. This keeps the moisture in and prevents overcooking. Lightly dust the layered fish fillets with flour. Salt and pepper the fish to taste.

In a large frying pan, heat the olive oil and 1 tablespoon of the butter over medium-high heat. Add the floured fish and cook quickly, turning the fillets over after about 2 minutes. Continue cooking until the fish flakes easily and looks opaque at its thickest point. While the fish is cooking, melt the remaining 2 tablespoons butter in a small skillet and toss the bread crumbs in the butter until golden. Serve the fish on a platter or on individual plates, topped with the buttered bread crumbs and surrounded by the lemon quarters.

Halibut Baked on Vegetables

(three or four servings)

A good, straightforward way to cook halibut with a few winter vegetables. Serve with Buttermilk Cornbread (see page 155).

2½ tablespoons butter, melted
About ¼ head cabbage, finely
  chopped (3 cups)
3 stalks celery, chopped
2 carrots, grated

1 pound fillet of halibut or
  other white fish (about
  4 fillets)
Salt and pepper to taste
1½ tablespoons lemon juice

Preheat the oven to 450°F.

Pour the melted butter into a 9-inch square baking dish. Layer the cabbage, celery, and carrots in the baking dish. Put the fish fillets on top of the vegetables in a single layer. Sprinkle with salt and pepper to taste and drizzle with the lemon juice. Cover the dish and bake for about 15 to 20 minutes (the time will vary depending upon the thickness of the fish fillets). The fish is done when the fillets have turned opaque at their thickest part. Serve directly from the dish.

Sweet Walnuts and Prawns

(four servings)

I love this dish. The slightly sweet walnuts and the peppy horseradish seem meant for each other. Serve Maple Persimmons (see page 230) for dessert.

Steamed Rice

2⅔ cups water	1⅓ cups long-grain white
1 teaspoon salt	rice (makes 4 cups cooked)

1 cup water	3 tablespoons cream-style
1 cup sugar	horseradish
1½ cups walnuts, in large	1 pound shrimp (about 20
pieces	large shrimp), cooked,
¾ cup mayonnaise	shelled, and deveined (see
2 tablespoons light corn syrup	page 19)

Using a deep heavy-bottomed pot, bring the 2⅔ cups water and salt to a boil. Add the rice slowly so the boiling doesn't stop. Cover and simmer for 20 minutes without stirring or removing the cover. Then check: the rice should be just soft and the water absorbed.

While the rice is simmering, preheat the oven to 350°F. Put the 1 cup water and sugar in a heavy-bottomed saucepan and bring to a boil. Add the walnuts and simmer for about 4 minutes. Drain and spread the walnuts in a single layer on a baking sheet. Put in the oven and roast for about 5 or 6 minutes. Watch carefully so the walnuts don't brown—you just want to dry them out. Remove from the oven and set aside.

Mix the mayonnaise, corn syrup, and horseradish together in a large bowl, stir until smooth and well blended, and set aside. Bring a pot of water to a boil, drop the shrimp in, and let simmer for about 30 seconds, just long enough to heat the shrimp through. Drain the shrimp and quickly stir them into the horseradish sauce, coating them on all sides. Fluff up the rice with a fork. Serve the shrimp with the sweet walnuts on top and the rice on the side. This dish is good served warm or at room temperature.

FLAVOR

The hardest thing to learn in cooking is how to give a dish the right tone of flavor. Flavoring a dish requires critical tasting and your full attention.

Even though recipes give specified amounts of herbs, spices, or aromatics, you can't depend on these ingredients being uniformly fresh. The flavors of ingredients kept in jars can vary from lots of "oomph" to almost no taste at all. One essential rule: Always taste each ingredient before adding it to your preparation, so you know how strong or weak it is, and if it still retains its good quality.

I use garlic, citrus, and ginger quite often to flavor food. If you chop these ingredients with salt or sugar the flavors are magically diffused throughout the dish. The salt and sugar crystals act like little missionaries, spreading the flavors.

To infuse garlic flavor: Put as many peeled garlic cloves as needed on a chopping board. Sprinkle coarse salt or regular table salt over the cloves (proportion the amount of salt used to the size of the recipe you're making). Chop the garlic cloves finely, or run them through a mini-processor until the garlic juice blends with the salt crystals. Add this mixture to your recipe and proceed. (The small jars of garlic salt, onion salt, and celery salt that you see in the markets are made using this general principle.)

Generally I use citrus zest and ginger in sweet dishes, so I mix these flavors with sugar. I put a portion of sugar and the ginger or citrus in the food processor or chop by hand. The flavors will be captured in the sugar crystals and then melted into the dish.

Laguna Beach Shrimp Curry

(six servings)

When I started making Laguna Beach Shrimp Curry, back in the 1940s, I first used Campbell's Cream of Tomato soup for the sauce. Later, a neighbor taught me how to make coconut-milk sauce, which seems more mellow with the shrimp. And it is nice to have the toasted coconut for a condiment. In those days around beach towns, shrimp was considered an economy food; they were as cheap as squid is today.

1 cup water	1½ tablespoons curry powder
1 cup milk	½ teaspoon salt, or to taste
1 cup grated unsweetened	2 teaspoons lemon juice
coconut	2 pounds shrimp, cooked,
5 tablespoons butter	shelled, and deveined
1 medium onion, chopped	(see page 19)
¼ cup flour	6 cups steamed long-grain
2 cups chicken broth	white rice (see page 55)
(see page 47), warmed	

Heat the water and milk in a saucepan until it begins to bubble. Add the coconut, stirring to mix, cover the pan, and remove from the heat. Let the mixture stand for 1 hour.

After an hour, drain and squeeze excess milk from the coconut, reserving both the coconut and the milk mixture. Toast the coconut by spreading it on a cookie sheet and broiling for about 5 minutes. Watch constantly so the coconut doesn't burn.

Melt the butter in a 10-inch frying pan, add the onion, and cook over medium heat until the onion is tender, about 5 minutes. Add the flour and stir until smooth. Slowly add the chicken broth, curry powder, and salt, and cook over medium-low heat until thick, stirring constantly. Slowly add about ⅔ cup of the coconut-milk mixture and the lemon juice. Add more of the milk if a thinner sauce is desired. Add the shrimp, heat through, and serve over the rice. Top with the toasted coconut.

Baltimore Crab Cakes

(makes eight 3-inch-wide ¾-inch-thick crab cakes)

If you love crab cakes, American history, and miles of green grass horse country, head for Maryland. I did and I found the best crab cakes at Faidley's, a food stall in the Lexington Market in Baltimore, the oldest market in the United States. Incredible crab cakes—moist, creamy, and full of the taste of crab. A large sign on the wall says that Faidley's makes them with backfin crab, mayonnaise, Dijon mustard, and saltine crackers. I experimented with these four ingredients until I came up with this example of Faidley's winning crab cakes. Serve the cakes with Coleslaw (see page 187), bread and butter, and ice-cold beer.

1 cup mayonnaise	2 tablespoons vegetable oil
1 tablespoon plus 1 teaspoon	Lemon wedges
Dijon mustard	Tabasco sauce
2 cups saltine cracker crumbs	
About ⅔ pound crab meat (2 cups)	

Put the mayonnaise and Dijon mustard in a mixing bowl and stir until well blended. Add 1 cup of the cracker crumbs and all the crab meat and mix well.

Put a large piece of waxed paper on the counter and spread the remaining 1 cup of cracker crumbs on top. Divide the crab mixture into 8 equal portions and pat each into a ball. Gently flatten each ball into a round cake about 3 inches in diameter. Lightly coat the top and bottom of each cake with cracker crumbs.

Heat a large skillet over medium heat and film the bottom with the oil. Place the cakes in the skillet and fry over medium heat for a minute or so on each side, until just golden. Serve hot with lemon wedges and Tabasco sauce on the side.

Salmon with Cucumber and Caper Sauce

(three or four servings)

Cucumber and capers give salmon a crisp texture and sharp acid taste that bring out the best in this rich fish. Salmon is more full-bodied than most fish and calls for a peppy accent. Cook an extra pound of salmon and use what is left over to make Salmon Salad Niçoise (see page 16).

About 2 pounds of salmon
   steaks (allowing 1 pound of
   leftover salmon for Salmon
   Salad Niçoise)

Cucumber and Caper Sauce

1 cucumber, peeled and seeded	1 tablespoon capers, drained
3 tablespoons butter	2 tablespoons finely chopped
Salt to taste	parsley
3 tablespoons water	

Rinse the salmon under cold running water. Lay the salmon on a rack that fits in a pot with a lid. Cover the salmon with salted water. Put on the lid and simmer for about 10 minutes, or until the meat loses its deep pink color.

While the salmon is cooking, make the sauce.* Dice the cucumber into small pieces. Melt the butter over low heat, add the cucumber, and salt lightly. Cook for about 2 minutes, stirring constantly. Add the water and the capers and stir to blend. Taste and add more salt if needed. Stir in the parsley and cook, stirring for a second or two. Remove the salmon from the pot and serve with the sauce.

*Or you can make the sauce earlier in the day and refrigerate it. Heat before serving with the salmon.

Scandinavian Salmon Sandwich

(two open-face sandwiches)

For a Scandinavian-style supper, serve this open-face sandwich on a board with a cold glass of beer and Chilled Marmalade Grapefruit (see page 229) for dessert.

2 tablespoons whipped cream
  cheese
2 tablespoons mayonnaise
A little milk to thin cream
  cheese
1 teaspoon chopped fresh dill,
  plus a few sprigs for garnish

Salt and pepper to taste
A few drops of lemon juice
½ cup cooked flaked salmon
  (see preceding recipe)
2 slices light rye bread

Put the cream cheese and mayonnaise in a bowl and beat until smooth. Add a little milk if the mixture is too thick and stiff to spread easily. Add the dill, salt and pepper, and lemon juice, and stir until mixed well. Add the salmon and mix well.

Spread the salmon mixture over each slice of rye bread, and garnish with fresh dill.

Tarragon Fish on Toast

(four servings)

This is a snap to make and therefore a good recipe for busy people. Serve with a bowl of chopped seeded cucumber and red onion with vinaigrette.

1 tablespoon salt	4 thick slices white bread
½ cup milk	Soft butter
1½ to 2 pounds white fish fillets, about ½ to ¾ inch thick, cut into serving pieces	1 teaspoon chopped fresh tarragon; or ½ teaspoon dried tarragon
1 cup dry bread crumbs	
3 to 4 tablespoons butter, melted	

Preheat the oven to 500°F.

Butter or grease a baking pan that is large enough to hold the fish in a single layer. Stir the salt into the milk until the salt has dissolved. Dip the fish fillets into the milk, then coat both sides of each fillet with the bread crumbs. Place in the prepared baking pan in a single layer and pour the melted butter over the fish. Bake about 10 to 12 minutes, or until the fish is opaque and flakes easily with a fork.

Meanwhile, prepare the toast: spread the slices of bread with soft butter, sprinkle the tarragon on top, and put in the oven on a baking sheet 5 minutes before the fish is done. When the fish and

toast are ready, remove the fillets from the baking pan with a spatula and arrange equal amounts on top of the toast. Pour any pan
juices over and serve.

Fish Tacos

(eight tacos, or four servings)

When Americans think of tacos, they almost never think of fish;
but corn tortillas with fish, seasoned with cumin, lime juice, and
cilantro, are typical Mexican tacos. Just about any kind of fish or
shellfish is good this way.

⅔ cup sliced scallions
6 medium tomatoes, diced
1 cup loosely packed chopped
  cilantro
Salt to taste
½ teaspoon ground cumin
1 pound white fish fillets
  (sole, halibut, snapper, cod,
  and so on)

2 tablespoons lime or lemon
  juice
4 tablespoons corn oil
8 tortillas (corn, flour, or
  whole wheat)

Toss the scallions, tomatoes, and cilantro in a bowl and add salt to
taste. Set aside.

Sprinkle salt and the cumin evenly over one side of the fish fillets, and drizzle the lime juice over the fillets. Heat a large skillet
over medium heat, film the bottom with 2 tablespoons of the corn
oil, add the fish, and cook until the fish is done, only a minute or
two, depending on the thickness of the fillets.

In another large skillet, heat the remaining 2 tablespoons of corn
oil and quickly fry the tortillas, one at a time, over medium-high

heat for a few seconds on each side. Drain on paper towels. Place a piece of fish on each tortilla, top with some of the tomato mixture, and serve at once.

Oyster Buns

(two to four servings)

Be prepared to make twice as many of these as you think people might eat. They'll ask for more.

4 round buns, about 3½ inches in diameter, cut in half (see Hamburger Buns, page 144)	⅓ cup cornmeal
	⅓ cup flour
	Pinch of cayenne pepper
⅓ cup Tartar Sauce (see page 162)	12 fresh oysters, shucked
	4 tablespoons (½ stick) butter
1 cup shredded iceberg lettuce	4 lemon wedges

Scoop out a small chunk of bread from the center of each bun half to allow room for the oysters. Spread each half evenly with Tartar Sauce and put some of the shredded lettuce on the bottom half of each bun.

In a dish or pie tin, mix together the cornmeal, flour, and cayenne. Pat the oysters dry, and roll each one in the breading mixture, coating it evenly. Put the butter in a frying pan over high heat. Quickly fry the oysters in the hot butter until golden on each side—this will take no more than 15 seconds on each side. Put the oysters on paper towels and pat to remove oil. Place 3 oysters on the lettuce and put the other half of the bun on top. Do not slice. Serve immediately.

Scallops with Corn and Cilantro

(four servings)

This is an unusual combination that captures some of the mysterious Mexican flavors that most of us love. The corn, cilantro, and
scallops complement one another, and the masa harina contributes
an earthy taste. Serve with warm tortillas and cold beer.

4 tablespoons (½ stick) butter
2½ cups corn kernels (if fresh
   is available, you will need 3 or
   4 large ears)
1 pound bay scallops
1½ cups milk
4 tablespoons masa harina
   (see Note, page 37)

Salt to taste
1 teaspoon (or more) hot
   pepper sauce
1 tablespoon lime juice
1 cup whole cilantro leaves
   (if not available, substitute
   ⅓ cup finely chopped
   scallions)

Melt the butter in a sauté pan. Stir in the corn and scallops and
cook for about 3 minutes, continuing to stir constantly. Remove
from the heat and set aside.

Put the milk in a small bowl and add the masa harina. Stir
briskly until the mixture is smooth. Put the sauté pan with the scallops over low heat and pour the milk mixture in, stirring constantly
until the sauce thickens. Taste and add salt as necessary and the hot
pepper sauce. Remove from the heat and just before serving stir in
the lime juice, then sprinkle the cilantro leaves over the top. Serve
with warm tortillas.

A French Country Supper

"I remember a meal that was unique.

It wasn't a lunch nor yet a dinner. Perhaps it was more a supper, served a little before five o'clock on the bluest afternoon of my life. I had lunched with my master in the country and he asked me to accompany him—for I practically never left him—to visit two old friends of his family, who lived in a little house in a big garden. An ancient servant opened the door and showed us into the drawing-room. Holland covers were on the furniture, an Empire clock had stopped on the mantelpiece, and through a high open door, I saw long shelves full of drying plums and apples.

The masters of this old abode came in arm-in-arm. They were a sweet old couple.

He was dressed in a frock-coat and grey trousers, she in a silk dress of the colour of dead leaves and of an antiquated cut. Only a big straw hat trimmed with a bunch of Mahon violets was lacking to make it a model of the fashion of 1830.

They faced us, rosy and fresh as the apples they preserved in the next room; they welcomed us, and immediately invited us to supper, for so they called the meal of which they partook at about half-past four in the afternoon.

What a pleasant little dolls' dinner party!"

—from *Clarisse, or
The Old Cook*

Chicken

Chicken Under a Brick

Roast Chicken with Smothered Potatoes

Chicken with Fresh Herbs and Potatoes

Chicken Sauté with Vinegar

Chicken Provençale

Mahogany Chicken Legs with Fresh Ginger

Smothered Chicken with Mushrooms

Hen Braised with Onions

Sara Tyson Rorer's Spanish Rice with Chicken

Lone Star Chicken

Chicken Succotash

Minced Chicken in Lettuce Leaves

Chicken Mock Hollandaise

I remember when I was first married I decided to buy a whole chicken and roast it. I dimly remembered that you were supposed to wash poultry, so I got a big bowl of sudsy water and gave the chicken a bath. I scrubbed the bird, rinsed, and dried it, and after it was roasted, I thought it was outstandingly good. However, when I told my neighbor that I had given my chicken a bath with Tide soap, she was appalled. It is not necessary to bathe your chicken, especially now that chickens are bathed for you on the production line.

Chicken used to be a very special and a rather expensive dish reserved for Sunday dinner. Today chickens are cheap and found everywhere, and of all the meats, chicken is probably the most popular.

Every now and then, someone starting a household who doesn't know much about cooking will ask me what she ought to cook for supper. I almost always reply, "Get a chicken and roast it." And if the cook is a real beginner, I add, "Be sure to take out the bag of giblets from the cavity." When I roast a chicken, I just rub it all over with oil, salt, and pepper, put it in a 400°F. oven, and then let it roast undisturbed, in a baking dish or a pan, for about forty-five to fifty-five minutes.

This chapter includes some exceptional chicken recipes in which chicken gets cut up and sautéed, smothered and braised, and flattened and fried. For example, there are two quick chicken sautés that are miles apart in flavor: Chicken Sauté with Vinegar (see page 75) is a smooth-tasting classic of subtlety (tarragon, tomato, wine vinegar . . .); Mahogany Chicken Legs with Fresh Ginger (see page 77) is a more bold-tasting dish (soy sauce and lots of fresh ginger). Here, too, is a rustic Italian way of frying chicken (Chicken Under a Brick) that results in a very crisp, juicy bird. Unlike chickens, any recipe in this chapter will fly.

Chicken Under a Brick

(four servings)

Weighting down a chicken while it fries is a wonderful Italian method that gives dramatic results. Your chicken will be very crisp on the outside and very juicy on the inside, and will taste of garlic, thyme, and olive oil. Serve with Garlic Rolls (see page 149), tomatoes, and Brown Sugar Custard (see page 227).

One 2½-pound frying chicken	Optional: red pepper flakes
3 tablespoons olive oil	3 tablespoons peanut oil
3 cloves garlic, chopped	
1 teaspoon dried thyme, crumbled	

Split the chicken down the back and remove the backbone. Flip the chicken over and remove its rib cage with a small sharp knife. Flatten the chicken with the heels of your hands. Mix together the olive oil, garlic, thyme, and optional red pepper flakes, and rub the mixture all over the chicken with your hands.

Heat the peanut oil in a 10- to 12-inch skillet over medium-high heat. Put the chicken in the skillet, skin side down. Rub any left-over olive oil mixture on the exposed side. Cover the chicken with foil, tucking the foil down around the chicken. Weight down with another, slightly smaller heavy skillet that has additional weights in it, such as bricks, a heavy rock, or another heavy pan. Press down firmly. Cook for 15 minutes, checking to make sure the chicken isn't browning too fast, lower the heat to medium, and cook 10 minutes more. Turn the chicken over, cover and weight down again, and cook for a final 10 minutes.

Roast Chicken with Smothered Potatoes

(four servings)

The reason the potatoes are called smothered here is because they are roasted under the flattened chicken, where they absorb all its juices. Try this with Tiny Herb Salads (see page 190) made with parsley and marjoram.

3 tablespoons olive oil	1 tablespoon chopped fresh
One 3-pound frying	rosemary; or 2 teaspoons
chicken	dried rosemary; plus fresh
Salt and pepper to taste	rosemary branches for
3 medium red onions, cut	garnish
into quarters	2 large cloves garlic, finely
8 new potatoes, cut in half	chopped

Preheat the oven to 425°F.
Film a 9 × 13-inch baking dish with 1 tablespoon of the olive oil.

Using a sharp knife or poultry shears, split the chicken down the back along the edge of the backbone. Then cut along the other side of the backbone and remove it. Remove the pads of fat from around the breast and the cavity.

Salt and pepper the red onions and the potatoes. Put the potatoes in the middle of the baking dish and sprinkle the rosemary and garlic over them. Flatten the chicken out over the potatoes, and surround with the onions. Drizzle and spread the remaining 2 tablespoons of olive oil over the chicken and then salt and pepper generously.

Put the chicken in the oven and roast for 45 to 50 minutes, or until the skin of the chicken is nicely browned. Pour off all the liquid and garnish with fresh rosemary branches. Serve hot or cold.

ROUSSEAU'S PARADOX

Jean-Jacques Rousseau observed that civilized man has become more and more separated from the world of home and family, orchards and farms, and all our deep, human links with life. He believed that sophistication, modernization, and urban life tend to corrupt the ideal integrity of the rural, simple, and traditional. "In every city dweller there is a displaced yearning for the rustic farm and land, the taste of the homegrown, all the natural foods. The paradox is that we do want authentic country flavors and integrity, but we do not seek the discomforts of the simple life, so we rediscover regionalism vicariously amid modern convenience and luxury." It is somehow both alarming and consoling to know that Rousseau wrote these words over two hundred years ago.

I think the best cure for this separation is home cooking. Looking for and buying raw ingredients, handling and preparing them in your familiar kitchen, and then eating at your own kitchen table will daily restore a feeling of connection with the natural world.

Chicken with Fresh Herbs and Potatoes

(four servings)

This is a rustic Italian dish from Irma Goodrich Mazza. She became a fine cook and cookbook author after she fell in love with a handsome Italian who taught her to cook with onions, garlic, olive oil, and herbs. This was long ago, when the average young American woman used only a hint of seasoning in her cooking.

One 3-pound frying chicken,
  cut into serving pieces
3 large russet potatoes, peeled
  and cut into 2-inch cubes
Salt and pepper to taste
3 tablespoons olive oil
3 tablespoons finely chopped
  parsley (Italian flat-leaf, if
  tender)

1½ teaspoons finely chopped
  fresh rosemary
2 cloves garlic, finely
  chopped

NOTE: Don't chop the herbs and garlic in a food processor—chop them by hand so they don't get soggy and wet.

Spread the chicken pieces and potatoes out on a piece of waxed paper and lightly salt and pepper on all sides.

Heat the olive oil in a large sauté pan. Add the chicken and potatoes and cook over medium heat until golden brown on all sides, moving and turning the pieces frequently. This will take about 10 minutes. Cover and lower the heat and cook 10 minutes more, or until the chicken is done. Remove the chicken and potatoes from the heat and put in a large serving bowl. Sprinkle the fresh herbs and garlic over the chicken and potatoes and toss until evenly distributed. Serve hot.

Chicken Sauté with Vinegar

(three or four servings)

Ideally, suppers should be made from things already in your kitchen and in this recipe everything but the chicken is probably on your shelf. Try making it the first time with red wine vinegar and the next using a less acidic vinegar such as rice vinegar: the dish will be much softer in flavor. Serve with plain buttered noodles, nicely peppered.

One 2½-pound frying chicken, cut into 8 serving pieces	1 tablespoon tomato paste
Salt and pepper to taste	½ teaspoon crumbled dried tarragon, or 1 teaspoon
4 tablespoons (½ stick) butter	finely chopped fresh tarragon
½ cup red wine vinegar	1 tablespoon minced parsley
¼ cup water	
1 teaspoon minced garlic	

Sprinkle the chicken with salt and pepper. Heat 2 tablespoons of the butter in a large skillet and put the chicken pieces in, skin side down. Brown on one side, turn over, and brown on the other. This takes about 8 minutes. Pour in half of the wine vinegar and all of the water, and cover. Turn the heat to low and cook about 10 to 15 minutes more. Check for doneness after 10 minutes—don't overcook. The chicken is done when the juices run clear when the flesh is pierced with a sharp knife.

Transfer the chicken to a platter and cover to keep warm. Add the garlic to the skillet and cook over medium heat for 1 minute. Add the remaining ¼ cup vinegar and boil quickly to reduce slightly, about 1 minute. Add the tomato paste, and the remaining

2 tablespoons of butter. Cook a few seconds, pour the sauce over the chicken, and sprinkle with the tarragon and parsley. Serve right away.

Chicken Provençale

(four servings)

A favorite recipe in James Beard's cooking classes during the 1970s was this rich, full-flavored blend of garlic, mayonnaise, and chicken, tempered and balanced with vinegar and lemon juice. (Don't worry—a whole head of garlic isn't too much; it mellows to just the right intensity during the slow simmering.) The dish is a meal in itself and needs only good peasant bread to round it out.

4 tablespoons olive oil
1 head of garlic, cloves separated and peeled
3 slices white bread, crusts removed
¼ cup red wine vinegar
Salt and pepper to taste
½ cup whole almonds
1 bay leaf, stem and vein removed, crumbled

3 whole chicken breasts, cut in half (making 6 halves)
1 cup chicken broth (see page 47)
½ cup mayonnaise
3 tablespoons fresh lemon juice

Heat 2 tablespoons of the olive oil in a large skillet over medium-high heat. Add the garlic and stir for about 1 minute, then remove and reserve. Soak the bread in the vinegar and season with salt and pepper. Lightly brown the bread on both sides in the skillet for 2 to 3 minutes, then remove and reserve. In a blender or food processor, put the garlic, bread, almonds, and crumbled bay leaf and process until you have a paste.

To the same large skillet add the remaining 2 tablespoons of olive oil and brown the chicken pieces on both sides; this takes about 8 minutes. Mix the garlic paste with the chicken broth, add it to the pan with the chicken breast side up, cover, and simmer about 20 minutes, or until the chicken is done.

Remove the chicken to a serving dish and cover to keep warm, leaving the sauce in the pan. Skim off and remove any excess fat with a spoon. Mix the mayonnaise and lemon juice together and gradually add to the pan, stirring it into the sauce. Pour the finished sauce over the chicken and serve.

Mahogany Chicken Legs with Fresh Ginger

(four servings)

Now you don't have to go to your favorite Chinese restaurant to enjoy the distinctive Asian tastes of this hard-to-flub recipe. I like this sauce best with dark meat, but you may use breasts or a whole cut-up chicken.

4 tablespoons peanut oil	⅓ cup sugar
8 chicken thighs and legs	½ cup sliced scallions
⅓ cup peeled and sliced	½ cup whole cilantro
(¼ inch thick) fresh ginger	leaves
⅓ cup soy sauce	4 cups steamed long-grain
⅓ cup sherry	white rice (see page 55)

Put the peanut oil in a deep skillet over medium-high heat. When the oil is hot, add the chicken pieces, skin side down, and the ginger slices. Brown the chicken for 10 minutes, then turn over and brown for 5 more minutes. (It is important to use a deep skillet because the chicken tends to spatter while browning.) Reduce the heat if necessary to keep the chicken and ginger from burning. If the ginger slices brown too quickly, remove them to a paper towel and put them back in the skillet when you add the soy mixture.

Mix together the soy sauce, sherry, and sugar. Pour the soy mixture over the chicken, cover, and cook for about 2 minutes. Transfer to a serving dish and garnish with the scallions and cilantro leaves. Serve immediately with the rice.

Smothered Chicken with Mushrooms

(four servings)

The old-fashioned version of this recipe added heavy cream at the end, but the dish doesn't need the extra calories: all the flavors are captured in the simple white sauce that binds together the delicate chicken flavor and the earthy mushrooms.

One 3-pound frying chicken, cut into serving pieces	4 tablespoons flour
Salt and pepper to taste	2 cups chicken broth (see page 47)
4 tablespoons olive or vegetable oil	1 pound fresh mushrooms, wiped clean and sliced
2 medium onions, chopped	¼ cup chopped parsley

Preheat the oven to 400°F.

Season the chicken pieces with salt and pepper. In a large heavy-bottomed skillet, heat the oil over high heat and brown the chicken pieces for 6 to 8 minutes, turning when necessary. Adjust the heat so that the chicken browns quickly, but does not burn. Transfer the chicken to a shallow casserole large enough to hold it in one layer.

Put the onions in the skillet and cook, stirring frequently, for about 5 minutes, or until they are soft and light colored. Stir in the flour and mix it well with a spoon. Pour in the chicken broth and, stirring constantly, let it come to a boil. Reduce the heat and let it simmer for 2 to 3 minutes. Pour the sauce over the chicken in the casserole, cover tightly, and bake in the oven for about 20 minutes.

Scatter the mushrooms over the chicken, re-cover, and bake for another 10 minutes, or until the chicken is tender. Sprinkle the parsley over the top and serve.

Hen Braised with Onions

(four servings)

Because this recipe is so easy, a child who is old enough to use a knife can enjoy making it. If there's any left over the next day, add some chicken broth and make the remains into a soup.

6 large yellow onions, sliced about ⅛ inch thick	1 cup water
1½ tablespoons ground ginger	Optional: 8 small red potatoes, unpeeled and cut in half
2 teaspoons salt	
1½ teaspoons pepper	Chopped parsley, for garnish
3 pounds chicken pieces: legs, thighs, breasts	

Put half the onion slices in the bottom of a Dutch oven, or in any heavy-bottomed pot with a lid. Mix together the ginger and salt and pepper, and spread out over a piece of waxed paper. Roll each piece of chicken in the seasoning mixture so that all sides are covered. Place the chicken pieces over the layer of onion slices and cover the chicken with the remaining onion slices.

Pour the water over all, and cover the pot with its lid. Braise over medium-low heat for 2 hours. If you're using potatoes, put them on top of the onions the last 30 minutes of cooking. Serve in bowls and sprinkle the top of each serving with chopped parsley.

Sara Tyson Rorer's Spanish Rice with Chicken

(four servings)

I adapted this recipe for Spanish rice from the one in *Mrs. Rorer's New Cookbook*, published in 1902. Sara Tyson was highly respected for her tasty dishes, and when I tasted her Spanish rice recipe, she didn't disappoint me. As she wrote at the end of the recipe, "If this dish is properly cooked and highly seasoned, this is a very delicious dish." True.

2½ cups water	1 teaspoon red pepper flakes
1½ cups tomatoes, broken up, with juice	2 large onions, chopped
	Salt and pepper to taste
3½ pounds chicken pieces: thighs, legs, breasts	1 cup chopped parsley
	1 cup long-grain white rice

Put the water, tomatoes with juice, chicken pieces, red pepper, onions, and salt and pepper in a heavy-bottomed pot with a lid. Bring to a boil and immediately reduce the heat to a simmer. Let simmer for 20 minutes, and turn the chicken pieces over. Add more tomato juice or water if too much liquid is evaporating and the chicken is drying out.

Add the parsley and rice, being sure there is a full 2 cups of liquid, and stir until mixed well with the other ingredients. Cover and simmer about 15 more minutes, checking once or twice to make sure the liquid hasn't all been absorbed by the rice: add more boiling water if it has. Taste and correct salt and pepper, and serve hot.

Lone Star Chicken

(four servings)

Don't be fooled by this ordinary-looking recipe: it's an outstanding dish, big and special, like the Lone Star State. Serve hot or cold. The recipe yields extra sauce (freeze it if not used within three days) that you can use later on other dishes, such as pasta.

18¾-ounce can solid-pack tomatoes	1½ teaspoons dried oregano, crumbled
1 large onion, chopped	2 tablespoons wine vinegar
4 cloves garlic, minced	Salt and pepper to taste
2 bay leaves	One 2½- to 3-pound chicken,
2 teaspoons ground cumin	cut into 8 pieces

Put the tomatoes and juice in a large casserole and break the tomatoes into bits. Add the onion, garlic, bay leaves, cumin, oregano, and vinegar, and stir to blend. Add salt and pepper. Simmer the sauce on top of the stove, stirring occasionally, for 30 minutes.

Preheat the oven to 350°F.

Add the chicken parts, pushing them down into the sauce. Cover the casserole and bake for about 1 hour.

Chicken Succotash

(six servings)

This old Southern recipe comes from Virginia, where it was first made over a hundred years ago. What is left of the old recipe is the corn and lima beans (the original meat used was squirrel). Serve with warm Buttermilk Cornbread (see page 155) and honey; have Wine Jelly (see page 225) for dessert; and you'll have a Southern-style supper.

4 to 5 pounds chicken pieces
2 teaspoons salt
2 medium fresh tomatoes, chopped; or 1 cup canned tomatoes
2 onions, thinly sliced
1 cup frozen green lima beans
3 potatoes, peeled and diced
1 cup corn kernels (fresh, frozen, or canned and drained)
1 teaspoon sugar
⅛ to ¼ teaspoon cayenne pepper

Put the chicken pieces in a large pot with the salt and water to cover. Bring to a boil and simmer for 40 minutes.

Preheat the oven to 350°F. Remove the chicken from the pot, reserving the broth. Take the meat from the bones, and set aside. Put the tomatoes, onions, lima beans, potatoes, corn, sugar, and cayenne pepper in a large casserole. Add the reserved broth, cover, and bake for 30 minutes.

Stir the chicken meat into the casserole and bake for another 10 to 15 minutes, uncovered. Taste and add more salt and cayenne pepper, if necessary. Serve hot.

Minced Chicken in Lettuce Leaves

(four servings)

Minced squab is a recipe from Mandarin China that is equally good made with chicken. Because iceberg lettuce is sturdy it makes the perfect wrapping for the warm filling. Serve with a big cup of Chinese Hot and Sour Soup (see page 42).

3 tablespoons vegetable oil
About 1 pound chicken
   breast, finely chopped
   (1⅓ cups)
1 small green bell pepper,
   seeded and finely chopped
1 teaspoon sugar
1 teaspoon salt

Pepper to taste
2½ tablespoons peeled and
   finely chopped fresh ginger
1½ tablespoons soy sauce
3 tablespoons water
1 tablespoon lemon juice
½ cup finely chopped walnuts

Sauce
½ cup rice vinegar
½ tablespoon soy sauce

1 teaspoon sesame seed oil
Hot sauce to taste

8 whole iceberg lettuce leaves,
   trimmed and chilled

To prepare the filling, heat the oil in a medium skillet, and add the chicken, bell pepper, sugar, salt, and pepper. Stir constantly over medium-high heat until the bell pepper turns a deeper green, about 2 to 3 minutes. Add the ginger, soy sauce, water, lemon juice, and walnuts, mix well, and cook a few seconds more. Remove the filling from the heat and put into a bowl.

To prepare the sauce, stir together the vinegar, soy sauce, sesame seed oil, and hot sauce until well mixed.

To assemble, put 3 or 4 tablespoons of filling on a lettuce leaf, spoon a little sauce over, and roll up the leaf. Serve hot or cold.

Chicken Mock Hollandaise

(four servings)

Mock hollandaise is hollandaise sauce made with chicken broth instead of melted butter. Serve this dish with asparagus and Popovers (see page 150).

4 tablespoons (½ stick) butter	Grated rind from 1 lemon
2 tablespoons minced onion	1½ tablespoons lemon juice
6 tablespoons cornstarch	3 cups diced cooked chicken
3 cups chicken broth (page 47)	8 ounces dried egg noodles
	2 egg yolks, lightly beaten
1 or 2 stalks celery, chopped (¾ cup)	Salt
	Pinch of cayenne pepper

Bring a large pot of water to the boil. Meanwhile, melt the butter in a medium-size heavy-bottomed saucepan and add the onion. Cook over medium heat, stirring, until soft. Stir in the cornstarch and cook over medium-low heat until smooth and blended. Slowly add the chicken broth, celery, lemon rind, lemon juice, and chicken. Cook, stirring, for 3 to 4 minutes. Remove from the heat, cover, and set aside.

Cook the noodles in the boiling water for about 8 minutes. While they are cooking, put the yolks into a small bowl and beat in ¼ cup of the hot sauce. Add the yolk-sauce mixture to the rest of the sauce in the saucepan. Cook for 1 minute more, and add salt and cayenne to taste. Drain the noodles and serve with the chicken and sauce on top.

Meat

Beef
Speed Steaks
Theater Steak
Beef Stroganoff
Tri-Tip Pot Roast
Stuffed Cabbage Rolls
The Perfect California Hamburger
Holey Moley Tamale Pie
American Meatloaf

Lamb
Ireland's Irish Stew
Shepherd's Pie
Applesauce Lamb Curry

Pork
Black Pepper Ribs
Pork Tenderloin with Jalapeño Sauce
Pork with Sage and Brown Rice

We Americans are just not the meat-and-potatoes people we once were. Chicken, fish, vegetables, grains, and beans have moved ahead in popularity, and meat no longer has the number-one status. Without consciously thinking about it, I find that I eat less meat too, and I don't know why. Maybe it's because meat doesn't taste as flavorful as it used to. Today's meat comes from pigs and cattle that are slimmer, trimmer critters than they used to be. They've been engineered to grow up faster and leaner, and they tasted better to me when they were a little less streamlined.

Still, my all-time favorite supper is a hamburger. It is a perfect composition of meat and condiments and, ideally, a little salad, packaged between two halves of a bun. I think of hamburgers as being the classic regional food of Southern California, where I grew up. (Actually, they originated around 1850 aboard a German-American ship, but they were vastly different then— tough, dried chunks of meat cooked with a little onion.) Please note the small tribute I've written to the hamburger along with the recipe for the all-time best hamburger (see page 95).

There are also those moments when nothing is better than steak and onions. I've found a trick that I use when it is time for a steak. I buy a T-bone steak at my supermarket and ask the butcher to cut it horizontally in half lengthwise (so it is half as thick). I freeze each half separately. When it's time to fry the steak I don't thaw it. I put it in a very hot skillet, salt and pepper generously, and fry on one side only for two to three minutes. (I add a sliced onion to the skillet for the last minute or two.) Frying it frozen keeps the inside meat pink and juicy. (See Speed Steaks; recipe follows.)

Some of the recipes in this chapter make use of cooked meat. So if you do a roast of lamb, for instance, on the weekend, plan to have some left to make Shepherd's Pie (see page 100) or Applesauce Lamb Curry (see page 101).

Speed Steaks

(four servings)

Now you can halve your steak and eat it, too. It can be difficult to cook a thin steak so that it is rare on the inside and seared on the outside. The secret is to fry it while it is still frozen.

2 tablespoons vegetable shortening
2 T-bone steaks (approximately 1 pound each), each cut in half horizontally, lengthwise, so it is half as thick, all 4 halves wrapped and frozen separately (do not thaw the steaks)

Salt and pepper to taste
1 large onion, thinly sliced in rings

Heat a large skillet over high heat until very hot. Add the shortening and swirl it around to film the bottom of the skillet. Generously salt and pepper the steaks. Put them into the skillet and fry on one side only for 1 minute. Add the sliced onion and cook quickly for 1 to 2 minutes more. Turn the steaks over and count to 5. Remove the steaks; the centers should still be pink. Serve with the onion rings on top.

Theater Steak

(four servings)

A perfect small meal all in one dish. The texture of the bread is very important: it needs to be sturdy enough to hold up to the mushroom and steak juices.

5 tablespoons butter	Salt and pepper
2 large onions, cut into thin rings	4 thick slices white bread (homemade is perfect)
½ pound fresh mushrooms, wiped clean and sliced	2 bunches watercress, washed, dried, and stems removed
Two 8-ounce fillets of beef steak (about 1 to 1¼ inches thick), cut in half lengthwise	

Melt the butter in a large skillet. When hot, add the onions and mushrooms, and cook for about 2 minutes, stirring constantly, just until they are soft. Remove the vegetables to a warm plate. Turn the heat up to medium-high and fry the steak quickly. Salt and pepper each side, and fry until the desired doneness is achieved. (After cooking 2 minutes on each side, cut into the steak with the tip of a knife. If it looks rosy and you like your steak rare, remove from the pan, remembering that the steak will continue cooking. If you want your steak medium, cook another minute or two.)

Remove the steak from the skillet and keep warm with the vegetables. Quickly put the bread into the skillet and fry, turning it over once, so it sops up all the pan juices.

To assemble, put a slice of bread on each plate, and spoon over a quarter of the onions and mushrooms onto each slice. Pile some watercress on top, then top with the steak. Gently press down on the steak with a spatula so some of the warm juices drip down. Serve at once.

Beef Stroganoff

(six servings)

Named for a nineteenth-century Russian count, beef Stroganoff was popular in this country during the 1960s and 1970s, but our fickle, trendy eating habits have left it languishing. Aristocratic credentials aside, it is just plain delicious. It makes a good dinner for harried cooks, because once the beef and onions have been sliced, the dish can be ready to serve in twenty or thirty minutes. Customarily served with white rice, it is much better with narrow, quarter-inch-wide noodles. Even simpler, spoon the Stroganoff over toast. Serve a watercress salad on the side.

2 pounds fillet or tri-tip (triangle tip) of beef, cut into ½ × 2-inch strips	3 large onions, chopped
	1 pound fresh mushrooms, wiped clean and sliced
Salt and pepper to taste	2 cups beef broth
2 tablespoons vegetable oil	2 cups sour cream

Sprinkle the meat with salt and pepper. Heat the oil in a large heavy-bottomed sauté pan, add the meat, and cook for just 1 minute over medium-high heat. Add the onions and cook over low heat, stirring often, for 4 to 5 minutes. Stir in the mushrooms, then the beef broth, and reduce the heat to a simmer. Simmer for 15 to 20 minutes, stirring often, until the meat is tender. Taste and add more salt if needed.

Stir the sour cream briskly, then add to the beef mixture. Mix well, and allow the Stroganoff to thoroughly heat through. Serve at once.

Tri-Tip Pot Roast

(four to six servings)

The tri-tip (or triangle tip) is a small cut of beef from the bottom sirloin that is tender enough not to need long cooking. You end up with the same rich pot roast flavors that take two to three hours to produce with other cuts. Don't forget a jar of hot mustard on the side.

3 tablespoons vegetable oil	2 onions, halved
One 2½-pound tri-tip beef roast	5 carrots, peeled and cut into 2-inch lengths
Salt and pepper to taste	4 medium potatoes, peeled and cut into quarters
2 cloves garlic, chopped	
1 cup water	

Heat the oil in a heavy Dutch oven (with a lid), add the meat, salt and pepper liberally, and brown on all sides over medium-high heat. Add the garlic, water, and onions, reduce the heat, cover, and simmer for about 20 minutes.

Add the carrots and potatoes, re-cover, and cook for another 20 to 30 minutes. Serve on a large platter with the vegetables all round.

Stuffed Cabbage Rolls

(four servings)

On a chilly night, there can't be a nicer supper than cabbage rolls with a little sour cream, warm Applesauce (see page 179), and homemade Rye Crackers (see page 145). Since it is simple to make twice as much, double the recipe and freeze the extra cabbage rolls for another night.

1 large head savoy cabbage	1 teaspoon allspice
3 tablespoons butter	Salt and pepper to taste
1 medium onion, chopped	¼ cup brown sugar
2 cloves garlic, finely chopped	1½ cups steamed long-grain
2 cups tomato sauce, homemade	white rice (see page 55)
or canned	1 pound ground beef
¼ cup water	

Grease a 9 × 13-inch baking dish. Preheat the oven to 350°F.

Bring a large pot of salted water to a boil. Remove and discard the core from the cabbage and put the cabbage into the boiling water, cover, and let gently boil for 4 or 5 minutes. Drain well and set aside.

Melt the butter in a large saucepan, add the onion and garlic, and stir over medium heat, cooking only until the onion and garlic are soft, not browned. Add the tomato sauce, water, allspice, and salt and pepper to taste. Lower the heat, and let the sauce simmer for about 15 minutes. Taste and correct the seasoning. The sauce should be thickened, but not so thick that it "plops" when poured from a spoon.

Remove about 15 of the tougher outer leaves from the cabbage and set aside to be used for wrapping the rolls. Chop the remaining cabbage coarsely and spread over the bottom of the greased baking dish. Sprinkle the brown sugar over the chopped cabbage, and lightly salt and pepper.

Put three quarters of the sauce into a mixing bowl with the rice and beef and mix well. Divide the filling into approximately 12 parts and roll each portion in a cabbage leaf. Place each roll on the chopped cabbage, seam-side down. Spoon a little of the remaining sauce on top of each roll. Cover the top with the remaining coarser outer leaves. Bake for 1 hour, and serve.

"Supper, after all, is our most social meal and, of all the day's contacts (apart, at least, from acts of love), perhaps the most needingly personal one."

—from *Simple Cooking*
by John Thorne

The Perfect California Hamburger

(one hamburger)

1 sturdy, fresh, tender hamburger bun

3 to 4 tablespoons mayonnaise

4 tablespoons finely chopped onion

Vegetable oil or shortening

¼ to ⅓ pound fresh ground beef with ⅓ part fat

Salt and pepper to taste

⅓ cup shaved (chiffonade) clean, crisp iceberg lettuce

2 to 3 tablespoons sweet relish

Only if you must:

2 tablespoons ball-park mustard (no Dijon)

2 tablespoons ketchup

Cheese (only mild Cheddar, please)

Slice the hamburger bun in half. Stir the mayonnaise and onion together and spread on one half of the bun. Heat a skillet and film the bottom with a little shortening or oil. Lightly form the meat into a patty and put it into the hot skillet. Salt and pepper the top very liberally. Fry for 2 or 3 minutes (don't press down with a spatula because this will dry the meat). Turn the hamburger over and salt and pepper it again. Fry until cooked to your liking. Put the hamburger patty on the onion mayonnaise, and spread the other half of the bun with relish and whatever additional condiments you may be using. Spread the lettuce over, add a slice of cheese, if you must, and put the bun together.

THE PERFECT HAMBURGER

My hamburger credentials come from the home of the one and only authentic hamburger, which was developed in Glendale, California, in August of 1936. The originator of this perfect hamburger is Bob Wian, the man who turned one rickety hamburger stand into a chain of 1,136 Bob's Big Boy restaurants across the country.

In order to make this hamburger you must have the following ingredients. You cannot allow yourself any creative license.

1. One sturdy, fresh, tender bun. It must have good, sound construction to keep the hamburger intact. See my recipe on page 144.

2. Lots of mayonnaise. (A dry hamburger is not acceptable.)

3. If onion is desired, it must be chopped and stirred into the mayonnaise so it doesn't slide around and become unevenly distributed.

4. Freshly ground beef. It must come from a cut that has enough fat (at least one third) to make a moist patty. Form the patty very gently so that the meat just holds together. (When ground meat is pressed firmly the hamburger becomes dry and rather tough.) The patty must be salted well before cooking.

5. Clean, crisp, fresh iceberg lettuce, thinly shredded so that it can be evenly distributed.

6. A liberal spread of relish. (Bob made his own.)

7. If you must have cheese on this hamburger, only mild Cheddar, please.

I guarantee that if you make this hamburger once, you will never fall back into making or eating those gourmet beef sandwiches called hamburgers.

Holey Moley Tamale Pie

(six servings)

I always wanted to open a tamale shop called Holey Moley Tamales and serve this dish as the specialty of the house. It is one of the rare examples of a lot of ingredients making a better pie. Double the recipe, make two pies, and freeze one. Serve with tropical fruit such as pineapple, mango, or papaya, with a little coconut sprinkled on top.

4 cups water
1½ cups yellow cornmeal
2 cups cold water
3 teaspoons salt
¼ to ½ cup butter or lard
½ pound bulk sausage
2 tablespoons chili powder
¾ teaspoon ground cumin
1 clove garlic, minced
2 medium onions, finely
  chopped
1 small green bell pepper, seeded
  and chopped
2 stalks celery, finely chopped
1½ pounds ground beef

3 cups canned Italian plum
  tomatoes; or 4 cups peeled
  and seeded fresh tomatoes
  (1½ pounds)
2 cups corn kernels
  6 ears), frozen, or canned
  and drained
4 ounces canned mild green
  chile peppers, diced
Optional: 1 teaspoon minced
  jalapeño chile peppers
1 cup pitted ripe olives
6 ounces medium or sharp
  Cheddar cheese, grated (2
  cups)

Bring the 4 cups of water to a boil in a 3-quart kettle. Meanwhile, stir the cornmeal into the 2 cups of cold water (this helps prevent lumping), and then stir this into the boiling water. Continue to stir while the water returns to a boil. Turn the heat to low, stir in 1½ teaspoons of the salt and butter, cover, and simmer 30 to 40 minutes, stirring often. This will become very thick.

Meanwhile, in a kettle or large frying pan, mash the sausage and cook over medium heat until it begins to lose color. Add the chili powder and cumin, stir, and cook about 5 minutes. Add the garlic, onions, green pepper, celery, and remaining salt. Stir and cook until the vegetables are soft, about 3 to 5 minutes. Crumble the beef into the pan and mash and cook until the raw color disappears. Add the tomatoes, corn, green chile peppers, and the jalapeño peppers, if using, and let the mixture simmer for 15 to 20 minutes.

Preheat the oven to 350°F.

Grease or oil a large baking pan that is at least 10 × 14 × 2 inches. Spread two thirds of the cornmeal mixture on the bottom and sides of the pan. Spoon in the filling and distribute the olives evenly over. Spoon the remaining cornmeal over the top and sprinkle with the cheese. Bake for about 1 hour. If you make an extra tamale pie, freeze it unbaked.

American Meatloaf

(six servings)

I've been looking for the perfect meatloaf for years. Too many meatloaves are carelessly put together with too many unassimilated ingredients. This meatloaf is the all-time winner in my house. It is cooked freeform rather than in a loaf pan so that it browns on all sides. Ketchup and Worcestershire sauce are in every American larder, and it seems to me that they belong in an American meatloaf. Instead of serving with mashed potatoes, bake a few potatoes, carrots, and onions in the pan with the meatloaf.

2 tablespoons butter
1 large onion, finely chopped
2 to 3 medium carrots, finely
    chopped
2 to 3 celery stalks, finely
    chopped
1 pound ground beef (chuck or
    round)
2 boneless pork chops (about
    ½ pound), ground
3 cloves garlic, minced or put
    through a garlic press
1¼ cups fresh bread crumbs

Salt, at least 1 teaspoon, or to
    taste
Pepper to taste
¾ teaspoon nutmeg
⅛ teaspoon cayenne pepper
1½ teaspoons Worcestershire
    sauce
¼ cup tomato ketchup
⅔ cup water
Optional: potatoes, carrots,
    and onions to bake with the
    meatloaf

Preheat the oven to 350°F.

Melt the butter in a large skillet. Add the onion, carrots, and celery, and over medium-low heat cook until softened, stirring often, about 5 to 6 minutes.

In a large bowl, put the beef and pork, sautéed vegetables, garlic, bread crumbs, salt, pepper, nutmeg, cayenne, Worcestershire sauce, tomato ketchup, and water. Mix thoroughly with your hands. Gently pat the meatloaf into an oval-shaped mound in an 11 × 7-inch baking dish. (If pressed together too firmly, the meatloaf won't remain moist and tender.) Bake for 45 to 50 minutes. Feel free to surround your meatloaf with small whole onions and/or carrots and small new potatoes.

Ireland's Irish Stew

(six servings)

You will love this Irish stew even if you are Italian. It has the taste of the land—natural and inviting. Irish Soda Bread (see page 156) belongs with this stew.

2 pounds lamb for stewing,
  some fat removed, cut in large-
  bite size pieces
Salt and pepper to taste (be
  generous)
4 large onions, thickly sliced
8 medium potatoes, peeled and
  thickly sliced

2 tablespoons chopped fresh
  thyme; or 1 tablespoon
  crumbled dried thyme
2 cups water
3 tablespoons finely chopped
  parsley

Preheat the oven to 325°F.
  Spread the lamb pieces on a sheet of waxed paper and salt and pepper liberally. Do the same with the onions and potatoes. Put the potatoes, onions, and lamb in layers in a large heavy casserole, sprinkling the thyme over each layer, and starting and ending with potatoes. Add the water slowly, without disturbing the layers, cover the casserole, put in the oven, and bake for 2 hours. Sprinkle with parsley and serve in bowls.

Shepherd's Pie

(four servings)

The mashed potato crust on Shepherd's Pie makes it unlike any other dish I know. You may not remember it from your childhood, but it's never too late to introduce it and enjoy it. It is such a tasty way to use leftover lamb.

4 medium potatoes
Salt and freshly ground
  black pepper to taste
8 tablespoons (1 stick) butter
3 cups chopped cooked lamb
  (any leftover lamb will do)

2 large cloves garlic, peeled
1 medium onion, quartered
1 teaspoon crumbled dried
  rosemary
2 tablespoons flour
¾ cup beef broth

Peel the potatoes and cut them into quarters. Put them in a pan and just cover them with cold water. Bring to a boil and boil gently for 15 to 20 minutes, or until tender when pierced with a fork. Drain well. Add salt, pepper and four tablespoons of the butter, and mash by hand until the lumps disappear, or put through a ricer. Set aside.

While the potatoes are boiling, preheat the oven to 325°F. Mix together the lamb, garlic, onion, and rosemary. Put through a meat grinder twice or chop until fine in a food processor.

Melt the remaining 4 tablespoons of butter in a large skillet and stir in the flour. Cook for a few minutes over medium heat until smooth and blended. Slowly add the beef broth. Cook, stirring constantly, until the gravy is thickened. Cook at least 5 minutes to get rid of the raw flour taste. Remove from heat, add the lamb mixture, and stir to blend. Add salt and pepper to taste.

Spread the lamb mixture evenly into a 1½-quart casserole or

deep pie dish. Spread the mashed potatoes evenly on top to the edge of the casserole. Make a crisscross design with a fork. Bake for 45 to 50 minutes, or until the meat is bubbling hot and the potatoes are browned.

Applesauce Lamb Curry

(four servings)

I never saw a lamb curry with fresh applesauce in it before this one. The mild hint of apple sweetness blends nicely with the spiciness of the curry.

4 tablespoons (½ stick) butter
2 tablespoons curry powder
2½ teaspoons ground ginger
½ teaspoon salt
½ teaspoon allspice
½ teaspoon mace
¼ cup flour
1½ cups canned chicken broth

½ cup heavy cream
1½ cups Applesauce (see page 179)
2 cups sliced cooked lamb (for example, leftover roast leg of lamb), at room temperature
4 cups steamed long-grain white rice (see page 55)

In a medium-size saucepan, melt the butter. Add the curry powder, ginger, salt, allspice, mace, and flour and stir until smooth and well blended. Slowly stir in the chicken broth and cream, and cook over medium heat, stirring constantly, until thickened. Add the applesauce and cook for 2 minutes more. Serve on a platter, making a mound of hot rice and adding sliced lamb on top, with the sauce poured over.

Black Pepper Ribs

(four servings)

This recipe came from James Beard, who dearly loved ribs cooked
this way, as did all of us in his cooking classes. Many of us had
never had spareribs without barbecue sauce. Ribs roasted this way
are crisp around the edges and have a fine pork flavor. I am partial
to a little Rhubarb-Onion Relish (see page 176) on the side.

   3 pounds pork spareribs   Salt and pepper to taste

Preheat the oven to 400°F.

Put the spareribs in a baking pan large enough to accommodate
them in a single layer. *Generously* salt and pepper both sides and
bake for 30 minutes on each side—1 hour in all. Serve right away.

Pork Tenderloin with Jalapeño Sauce

(four servings)

This shocking-pink sauce with its bright, peppy flavor turns ordinary roast pork into a flavor fiesta. Serve with Buttermilk Cornbread (see page 155) and black-eyed peas.

Salt and freshly ground   6 tablespoons jalapeño jelly
  black pepper to taste   ⅓ cup sour cream
2 pounds pork tenderloins*

*The tenderloin is the tender cylindrical muscle, about 2½ inches in diameter and
about 7 inches long, from the inside of the pork loin.

Preheat the oven to 425°F.

Line a small roasting pan with heavy aluminum foil. Generously salt and pepper the tenderloins. Melt 3 tablespoons of the jelly in a small pan over low heat and brush over the top of each tenderloin.

Put the tenderloins in the roasting pan about 1½ inches apart, and roast until a meat thermometer registers 160°F, about 15 minutes (don't overcook; pork tends to become dry). While the pork is roasting, stir the remaining jelly into the sour cream.

When the pork is almost done, heat the jelly–sour cream sauce in a small pan over very low heat, until *just* warm. Remove the pork from the oven, slice the tenderloins on the diagonal into ½-inch medallions, and serve with the warmed sauce.

Pork with Sage and Brown Rice

(four servings)

It's surprising how good sage and brown rice are together. Add pork and you have a more substantial supper dish. Fried Apple Rings (see page 180) are a nice addition, and you might serve Wirtabel's Melon Chutney (see page 178) or Pike's Perfect Pickles (see page 170) alongside.

½ cup flour
½ teaspoon salt
⅛ teaspoon pepper
1 pound boneless pork (loin or shoulder), cut into bite-size pieces
4 tablespoons vegetable shortening

1 large onion, chopped
1 cup brown rice
2 teaspoons crumbled dried sage leaves
3 cups water
Optional: 1 cup raisins

Stir together the flour, salt, and pepper in a mixing bowl. Add the pork and toss to lightly coat the pieces. Shake free of any excess flour mixture. Heat 2 tablespoons of the shortening in a large skillet over medium-high heat. Add the onion and cook about 5 minutes, or until it is soft and golden brown. Add the pork and continue cooking and stirring until all the pieces are browned, adding more shortening if needed to prevent sticking.

Remove the onion and pork from the skillet and set aside on a plate. Add the remaining 2 tablespoons of shortening to the skillet, and melt over medium heat. Add the brown rice. Cook the rice until it is golden brown, about 7 minutes, stirring frequently. Put the onion and meat back into the skillet along with the sage, water, and the optional raisins. Bring to a boil, cover, reduce the heat to a simmer, and cook for 45 minutes or until the rice is tender and the water is almost gone. Taste and add more sage if too faintly flavored. Be sure to stir the rice occasionally so it doesn't stick to the bottom of the pan. Taste for salt and pepper and correct seasonings. Serve hot.

Mostly Vegetables

Southern Green Beans

Red Beans and White Rice

Boston Baked Beans

Bean Stew with Raw Onions

Green Peppers and Cheese

Filled Green Peppers

Baked Green Peppers with
Anchovies, Rice, and Dill

New Red Potatoes with
Rosemary

Idaho Sunrise

Eggs, Tomatoes, and Potatoes
with *Gremolata*

Eggplant Filled with Roasted
Vegetables

Winter Vegetable Cobbler

Vegetable Porridge

Mark Peel's Barley Risotto

Humble Rice

Creamy Rice

Spanish *Riso*

Marietta's Spaghetti

Iceberg Lettuce and Noodles

Pasta Shells, Mushrooms, and
Brown Butter

Macaroni and Cheese

Curried Macaroni

Custard Sandwich

Frieda and Elinor's Onion Pie

Papusas

Green Chile Pie

Potato and Pepper Frittata

Tomato Rarebit

Linda Sue's Tomato Stew

Bread and Bacon Pancake

Fifty years ago, if my mother had put a plate of vegetables with no meat in front of my father for dinner, he would have thought she was demented or that we had suffered some financial disaster he didn't know about. Actually, my husband would have thought the same thing a few dozen years back. Those were the meat and potato years: bacon for breakfast, cold meat for lunch, and a roast for dinner.

When I was growing up in a small foothill town in Southern California, it seemed as if there were only about five or six fresh vegetables in our grocery store: carrots, string beans, cabbage, lettuce, and corn, and maybe one or two others. Vegetables certainly played second fiddle in my mother's cooking. I know we had string beans because I can remember stringing them. And I know we had carrots, but always raw, because my mother had read in some government pamphlet that they were better for us that way. My Irish father considered corn-on-the-cob to be cattle fodder, so our table never saw an ear of corn. He said almost every other vegetable was rabbit food.

Times have changed. The produce departments in supermarkets are huge, and we have a vast variety of vegetables. Cooks from around the world have introduced us to tomatillos, gingerroot, chile peppers, bok choy, and cilantro, to name a few plant foods new to most of us, and our cooking is far more interesting because of them.

All the recipes in this chapter are main supper dishes, and all of them are vegetable dishes except for a few pasta and rice recipes. Many of them have been collected over the years from friends and strangers eager to share a favorite vegetable dish. Green Chile Pie (see page 135) came from a county fair winner long ago. Linda Sue's Tomato Stew (see page 138) came from a photographer who doesn't cook except once in a while when she's homesick for this dish from her childhood. And Frieda and Elinor's Onion Pie (see page 133) came from the Swiss Alps by way of an Idaho housewife.

Southern Green Beans

(four servings)

For the last few years most of us have been following the recommended way of cooking green beans until *just* tender, because we believed that long cooking destroyed flavor and vitamins. But Southern Green Beans with potatoes and a hint of bacon have a fullness of flavor and depth of character that crunchy beans don't have. Serve with warm cornbread.

3 or 4 slices smoky-style bacon, diced	Salt and pepper to taste
	1 cup water
1 pound green snap beans, washed, ends trimmed, and cut into 1-inch lengths	2 scallions, sliced
	2 medium potatoes, peeled and diced

Heat a Dutch oven or heavy-bottomed pot with a lid. Add the bacon, and cook over medium-low heat until lightly brown, about

5 minutes. Add the green beans, salt and pepper, and water. Cover and cook for about 10 minutes over medium-low heat. Add the scallions and potatoes, stir to mix, cover, and cook for 30 minutes more. Check once or twice to make sure the liquid hasn't all evaporated. Serve hot.

FARMERS' MARKET

A visit to the farmers' market can be as inspiring and as uplifting as a trip to Yosemite. If you've never eaten fruit that has been tree ripened, or cooked vegetables at their peak of maturity, you can't imagine what you've been missing. Going to the farmers' market, walking from stand to stand, and talking to friendly people is a very pleasant experience.

Supermarkets, with their vast array of foods, are fascinating and indispensable, but a farmers' market, with fewer foods to buy, all of them fresh and sold by their growers, is so much more personal. There's an appreciation at my supper table when the dishes have been made from the produce of farmers I know.

Often you'll find people exchanging recipes at the market and that can be rewarding. I usually return home each week with some cooking tip or a fresh herb to cook a new way with a favorite vegetable. Some of the recipes I collected at the farmers' market are Wirtabel's Melon Chutney (see page 178), Green Peppers and Cheese (see page 113), and New Red Potatoes with Rosemary (see page 116).

Red Beans and White Rice

(six servings)

Beans and rice are oddly delicious together. You may approach this Creole dish with low expectations, but once you've tried it, you'll see why it's a beloved staple in the South. The nutritionists keep telling us to put more legumes and grains in our diets, and I can't think of a better way to do that than serving red beans alongside white rice.

2 cups (about 1 pound) dried
red beans, soaked overnight
(see page 18)
1 carrot, peeled and diced
1 large onion, chopped
¼ cup chopped celery with
leaves

1 bay leaf
2 teaspoons Tabasco sauce
1 pound salt pork, diced
Salt and pepper to taste
2 cups steamed long-grain
white rice (see page 55)

Drain and rinse the beans, return them to the pot, and add the carrot, onion, celery, bay leaf, Tabasco sauce, and salt pork. Add enough water to cover, bring to a boil, reduce the heat, and simmer for about 2 hours, or until the beans are tender. Some of the beans should be mushy. Add more water if necessary, or mash some beans to thicken. Salt and pepper to taste, being careful not to oversalt. Serve the beans in the same bowl with the rice, side by side.

Boston Baked Beans

(four servings)

I don't think Bostonians bake their beans overnight in the ashes of their fireplaces anymore, but Boston baked beans still need to be long cooked to have that rich, mellow flavor that only long, slow cooking creates. Once you have quickly assembled the dish and put the beans in the oven, they don't need you, except to check up hourly to see if more liquid is needed. This dish can be made on a Sunday and reheated. Serve with Piccalilli (see page 177) and Coleslaw (see page 187).

2 cups Great Northern beans, or small dried white beans, soaked overnight (see page 18)
2 teaspoons dry mustard
3 tablespoons dark brown sugar

3 tablespoons molasses
¼ pound salt pork, cut into ½-inch cubes, leaving the bottom attached to the rind

Preheat the oven to 325°F.

Drain the beans, cover with fresh water, and cook until tender, about 1 hour. Drain, reserving the liquid. Stir together the mustard, brown sugar, molasses, and 2 cups of the reserved liquid. Put the salt pork in a 2-quart bean pot or casserole, add the beans, and then add the molasses mixture. Stir to blend. Cover and bake for 5 to 6 hours. They are done when soft. Check every hour or so to make sure the beans don't dry out. Add more of the reserved liquid, or water, as needed to keep the beans moist. Taste and correct seasonings. Serve hot.

Bean Stew with Raw Onions

(four servings)

Adding fresh raw onions to this dish just before you serve it boosts the taste and texture. Make this bean stew and taste it before and after you add the chopped raw onion: you will be surprised by the difference.

1¼ cups dried red or pinto
 beans, soaked overnight (see
 page 18)
6 slices bacon
8 cups water
1 large onion, chopped
 (1 cup)
3 stalks celery, chopped

1 cup chopped parsley
⅓ cup yellow cornmeal
⅛ to ¼ medium head cabbage,
 chopped (2 cups)
1½ teaspoons ground sage
1½ teaspoons salt
2 medium onions, chopped
 (1½ cups)

Drain the beans. Put aside 1 slice of bacon and dice the rest. In a large (5-quart) soup pot, put the beans, diced bacon, and water. Bring to a boil and cook over low heat for 30 minutes.

In a frying pan, cook the remaining bacon slice until crisp. Remove from the pan, crumble, and set aside. Add the 1 cup chopped onion, celery, and parsley to the bacon drippings. Sauté the vegetables over medium heat until soft, about 5 minutes.

Add the cornmeal to the beans and bacon in the soup pot, and stir to mix. Add the sautéed vegetables, cabbage, sage, and salt, and stir. Cover and cook for 30 more minutes. Just before serving, stir in the 1½ cups chopped onions or sprinkle the onions on top of individual servings with the crumbled bacon. Serve hot.

Green Peppers and Cheese

(four servings)

One Saturday at the farmers' market I was buying some Anaheim chiles and the woman next to me asked me if I had ever made Peppers and Cheese. "It's so simple," she said. "Do try it!" I did, and she was right.

2 tablespoons olive oil
8 Anaheim or California chile
  peppers,* split, seeded, and
  deveined
6 ounces Monterey Jack,
  fontina, or Gouda cheese,
  sliced

1 large onion, finely chopped
2 tablespoons corn oil
8 tortillas (corn, flour, or
  whole wheat)
Fresh cilantro

Heat the olive oil in a frying pan. Put in the peppers, open and skin sides down, and flatten them with a spatula as they cook. Cook over medium heat for about 5 minutes, or until the skins are blistered and browned. Put 1 slice of cheese and 2 tablespoons of onion in each pepper. Fold the pepper over the cheese and cook over low heat 1 minute, then remove from the heat. Warm the tortillas by putting two at a time in a steamer over boiling water. Leave only for a few seconds. Remove and keep warm in a covered dish. Put a filled pepper and a few sprigs of cilantro into each warm tortilla and fold the tortilla in half. Serve hot.

*Anaheim peppers are about 6 inches long, light green, and about 1½ inches in diameter. They are one of the milder peppers. The hottest and least flavorful parts, the seeds and veins, are almost always removed before cooking.

Filled Green Peppers

(four servings)

In the summertime, all the ingredients for this dish will be at the farmers' market. The quality of the tomatoes is important, and for a short time in the summer they will be perfect: sweet, acidic, firm, juicy, and bright red. This is a very practical dish: the filled bell pepper halves are easy to pick up and eat cold on a picnic, yet they are just as good served hot on a plate. Serve a sharp, creamy cheese, green onions, and whole wheat bagels on the side.

4 green bell peppers, halved lengthwise, seeded, and deveined	1 small eggplant, chopped
	1 tablespoon chopped fresh oregano; or 1½ teaspoons dried crumbled oregano
2 tablespoons olive oil	Salt to taste
3 cloves garlic, finely chopped	Generous amount of pepper
1 large onion, chopped	Fresh basil leaves, for garnish
2 medium tomatoes, peeled and chopped	

Preheat the oven to 350°F. Film a 9 × 13-inch Pyrex baking dish with olive oil.

Put the peppers into a pot of salted, boiling water; place a plate in the pot on top of the peppers to keep them under the water; and parboil for 4 minutes. Remove and set aside.

Film a sauté pan with the olive oil and heat. Add the garlic and onion and cook over medium heat for a minute or two, just to soften. Add the tomatoes, eggplant, oregano, salt, and pepper. Stir to mix and blend thoroughly. Taste for salt and correct if neces- sary. Cover the pan and cook over medium-low heat for 10 minutes, stirring once or twice. Uncover and cook another 3 minutes, stirring often. Remove from heat.

Put the pepper halves in the prepared baking dish. Using a slotted spoon, fill the halves with the tomato/eggplant mixture. Bake for 20 minutes. Remove and serve hot or cold, with whole, fresh basil leaves on top.

Baked Green Peppers with Anchovies, Rice, and Dill

(four servings)

Unless you know you love anchovies, this dish may not be for you. The pepper halves are filled with the brazen flavors of olives, garlic, lemon, dill, and salty fish.

4 green bell peppers, cut in
  half lengthwise, stemmed,
  seeded, and deveined
2-ounce can anchovy fillets,
  packed in oil
2 tablespoons finely chopped
  onion
3 cloves garlic, minced
1½ tablespoons chopped
  fresh dill

2 tablespoons chopped parsley
3 cups steamed long-grain
  white rice (see page 55)
2 tablespoons lemon juice
3 tablespoons olive oil
Pepper to taste
12 whole black olives

Preheat the oven to 350°F.

Bring a large pot of water to a boil. Put the pepper halves in the boiling water; place a plate in the pot on top of the peppers to keep them under water; and blanch them for about 4 minutes, or until they are just cooked and slightly soft. Remove the peppers from the water and set aside.

Drain the anchovies and put the anchovy oil in a skillet over medium heat. Add the onion and garlic and cook until soft, but not browned. Add the dill and parsley and stir until blended. Remove from the heat. In a bowl, mix together the onion mixture, rice, lemon juice, olive oil, pepper, black olives, and half the anchovy fillets (or more if you wish). Fill the pepper halves with the mixture and place them in an oiled baking dish. Cover and heat in the oven for about 20 minutes, or until heated through. Serve warm.

New Red Potatoes with Rosemary

(four to six servings)

I first had tiny red new potatoes fixed this way at a cocktail party and watched platter after platter disappear. Everyone loved them. This is also a dandy dish for supper with scrambled eggs, cottage cheese, or cold chicken.

4 pounds tiny red new potatoes (approximately 60), about 1½ inches in diameter, unpeeled
¼ cup olive oil
3 teaspoons kosher salt

4 tablespoons fresh rosemary leaves; or 2 tablespoons crumbled dried rosemary leaves; plus some rosemary branches, for garnish

Preheat the oven to 350°F.

Put the potatoes in a large bowl and toss with the olive oil, salt, and rosemary leaves. Put the potatoes in a roasting pan, and put them in the oven for about 30 minutes, until just done in the center when pierced with a fork. Serve on a platter, surrounded by rosemary branches.

Idaho Sunrise

(one serving)

This is simply a baked potato with a bright yellow egg sitting on top of it, but when you mash the egg into the buttered potato it's like the sun coming up over the mountains.

1 medium baking potato (Idaho or russet Burbank), about ½ pound	Salt and pepper to taste
1 tablespoon butter plus 1 teaspoon melted butter	2 tablespoons milk 1 egg

Preheat the oven to 450°F.

Scrub the potato and then dry it. Pierce with a fork, put in the oven, and bake for about 40 to 50 minutes, or until it feels soft when pierced with a small knife.

Remove from the oven, and, using a potholder to hold the hot potato, slice a piece off the potato lengthwise, large enough so you can scoop out the insides. Put the scooped-out potato in a small bowl, add the 1 tablespoon butter, salt and pepper, and milk, and mash with a fork, mixing well.

Refill the potato shell. Put the filled potato on a pie plate or baking sheet. Break the egg and drop it on top of the potato, spoon the teaspoon of melted butter over the egg, salt and pepper it, and put in the oven. Bake for about 8 to 10 minutes, or until the egg is set but the yolk is still soft enough to make a nice sauce for the potato. Serve hot.

Eggs, Tomatoes, and Potatoes with Gremolata

(four servings)

The combination of lemon zest, parsley, and garlic is called *gremolata* in Italy. Have some chunks of bread on the side to dunk in the extra *gremolata*. Drink a glass of strong iced espresso for dessert with Plain Jane Sugar Cookies (see page 209).

1½ pounds small new red
   potatoes, about 1½ inches in
   diameter, unpeeled
8 eggs
½ cup olive oil
2½ teaspoons finely chopped
   lemon zest

2½ tablespoons finely
   chopped parsley
4 teaspoons finely chopped
   garlic
4 medium tomatoes, each
   cut into 6 wedges
1 teaspoon kosher salt

Put the potatoes and eggs in a large pot of salted water. Bring to a boil and cook about 12 minutes, or until the potatoes are tender when pierced with a knife.

While the potatoes and eggs are cooking, mix the olive oil, lemon zest, parsley, and garlic together. Drain the potatoes and eggs and let cool slightly. Shell and quarter the eggs.

While they are still warm, put the potatoes and eggs and the tomatoes in a large bowl, and add the salt. Add a little more than half the *gremolata* and toss to coat the potatoes, eggs, and tomatoes thoroughly. Put the remaining *gremolata* in a small bowl to pass at the table.

Eggplant Filled with Roasted Vegetables

(four servings)

All the ingredients in this recipe come together like a good jigsaw puzzle. Every part fits and everything gets used: the roasted egg-plant pulp makes the relish and the relish completes the dish.

1 large long eggplant (or 2 small ones)

1 pound zucchini, chopped into ½-inch chunks

1 pound yellow crookneck or pattypan squash, chopped into ½-inch chunks

2 onions, chopped

Salt and pepper to taste

2 teaspoons crumbled dried marjoram

6 tablespoons olive oil

3 cloves garlic, finely chopped, or put through a garlic press

1 cup finely minced parsley

2 medium tomatoes, finely chopped

½ teaspoon cayenne pepper

Preheat the oven to 350°F.

Slice the eggplant lengthwise and place on a baking sheet, cut side down. On another large baking sheet, spread the zucchini, squash, and onions. Salt and pepper liberally, and sprinkle the mar-joram and 3 tablespoons of the olive oil over the mixture. Using your hands, toss and mix on the baking sheet, spreading the vegeta-bles evenly over the sheet. Put the eggplant and vegetables into the oven and set the timer for 30 minutes. Check eggplant for doneness by piercing the center with a fork; it should be tender. Remove the eggplant, but continue to cook the remaining vegetables for 15 to 20 minutes more, or until slightly brown on top. Remove from the oven and set aside.

While the vegetables finish baking, make the relish. Spoon out the pulp from the eggplant, leaving ¼ inch of pulp attached to the skin. Process the pulp in a food processor or finely chop it by hand. Put the eggplant pulp in a mixing bowl and add the garlic, parsley, tomatoes, salt, cayenne pepper, and the remaining 3 table-spoons of olive oil. Mix well, taste, and add salt and more cayenne if needed. Cut the eggplant shells in half so there are 4 sections. Divide the roasted vegetables into four portions and fill each shell. Put about ½ cup of relish beside each portion of filled eggplant. Serve hot or cold.

Winter Vegetable Cobbler

(six servings)

People get excited when they hear the name Winter Vegetable Cob-bler, and nobody yet has been disappointed after making it.

1 turnip, peeled and cut into
   bite-size wedges
1 potato (russet or baking),
   peeled and diced
1 celery root, peeled and diced
   (about 1½ cups)
1 onion, coarsely chopped
3 carrots, peeled and sliced

½ cup chopped parsley
1 cup chicken broth (see page
   47)
1 tablespoon cornstarch
1 teaspoon salt
Freshly ground pepper to taste
4 tablespoons (½ stick) butter

Cobbler Dough
1¾ cups flour
1 tablespoon baking powder
½ teaspoon salt

6 tablespoons (¾ stick) butter,
   chilled and cut into pieces
¾ cup heavy cream

Preheat the oven to 325°F.

Put the turnip, potato, celery root, onion, carrots, and parsley in a 2-inch-deep, 3-quart ovenproof baking dish (I use an approximately 13 × 9 × 2-inch Pyrex baking dish). You should have about 6 cups of vegetables. In a small mixing bowl, blend the chicken broth with the cornstarch. Pour over the vegetables and mix well. Add the salt and pepper and mix to blend. Dot the top of the vegetables with the butter.

Mix the flour, baking powder, and salt in a large mixing bowl and stir with a fork to blend. Put the pieces of chilled butter into the flour mixture and rub quickly with your fingertips until the mixture resembles coarse crumbs. Using a fork, slowly stir in the cream, until roughly mixed. Gather the dough into a shaggy mass and knead 5 or 6 times. Roll out the dough on a lightly floured board until it is the size of the top of the baking dish. The dough should be about ¼ inch thick.

Place the dough on top of the vegetables. Bake for 55 to 65 minutes, until the vegetables are cooked through and the crust is browned. Test vegetables for doneness with a knife tip or skewer. Remove from the oven and serve hot.

Vegetable Porridge

(four servings)

I love the word porridge, but lots of people don't. To me, the word sounds wholesome and comforting. Here it stands for a flavorful dish of oats, barley, and vegetables. Even though everyone doesn't love the name, everyone loves the dish.

2 tablespoons butter
1 large yellow onion, chopped
3 carrots, peeled, halved, and
   sliced
3 stalks celery, sliced
8 cups chicken broth (see page
   47)

1 cup pearl barley
Salt and pepper to taste
2 zucchini, sliced ¼ inch
   thick
1 cup firmly packed fresh
   spinach, washed
½ cup rolled oats

Melt the butter in a 5-quart heavy-bottomed soup pot, and add the onion, carrots, and celery. Cook over medium heat, stirring often, for 5 minutes. Add the chicken broth, barley, and salt and pepper. Simmer for 1½ hours, or until the barley is tender, stirring every so often so the barley does not stick to the bottom of the pot.

   Add the zucchini, spinach, and oats. Simmer for another 10 minutes. Taste and correct the seasonings. Serve hot.

Mark Peel's Barley Risotto

(four servings)

Mark Peel, the chef of Campanile Restaurant in Los Angeles, made up this dish, which is greater than the sum of its parts. This is a speedy risottolike dish. Intermingled, the earthy flavors of mushrooms, barley, and rice taste unexpectedly new and different.

½ cup barley
½ cup short-grain rice
3 tablespoons butter
½ pound mushrooms, wiped
　　clean and sliced (3 cups)

½ cup chicken broth (see
　　page 47)
Salt to taste

In a large (at least 2-quart) pot, bring 6 cups of salted water to a boil. Add the barley and rice and let simmer for 25 minutes, or until tender. Drain any water that remains after the barley and rice are cooked.

Melt the butter in a large skillet. Add the mushrooms and slowly cook over low heat for about 7 to 10 minutes. Mix in the cooked barley and rice and the chicken broth. Salt to taste and serve.

"In our family, we have always found that eating together aids family solidarity. When we face serious problems, we have a way of saying, 'Well, let's have supper first.' We find that tensions ease and difficulties can be handled after we have gathered around the table and had a good meal."

—from *My Own Cook Book*
by Gladys Tabor

Humble Rice

(four servings)

Humble Rice is a thin layer of rice and vegetables that turns golden and crisp on top when baked. If you like crunchy rice, then this is your kind of recipe.

3 tablespoons olive oil
2 cups steamed long-grain
   white rice (see page 55)
2 medium tomatoes, cut into
   bite-size pieces

2 small zucchini, cut into bite
   size pieces
1 cup whole pitted black
   olives
Salt and pepper to taste

Preheat the oven to 350°F.

Spread 1½ tablespoons of the olive oil in the bottom of an 11 × 17-inch baking dish. Toss the rice, tomatoes, zucchini, and olives together and spread in a thin layer in the baking dish. Drizzle the remaining 1½ tablespoons of olive oil over the top. Add salt and pepper. Bake for 30 to 40 minutes.

Creamy Rice

(four servings)

You have to try Creamy Rice at least once. It's thick and thin at the same time, and it can be eaten both in winter and in summer. It's the all-purpose dish! Try it with a small dish of buttered green peas or a piece of braised fish. Put a little Creamy Rice aside, add some sugar and a few raisins, and there's your dessert.

4 cups water	2 teaspoons lemon juice
1 teaspoon salt	½ teaspoon grated or ground
½ cup long-grain white rice	nutmeg
2 tablespoons butter	1½ teaspoons grated lemon
3 tablespoons flour	zest
4 cups milk	

Put the water and ½ teaspoon of the salt in a 5- or 6-quart pot. Bring the water to a boil and slowly pour in the rice; shake the pot to level the rice, and reduce heat to a simmer. Cook the rice (be sure the water is bubbling) for 15 minutes, stirring often. After 15 minutes, the rice should be soft and there should be some liquid left in the pot. Remove from the heat and set aside.

Put the butter and flour in a 5- or 6-quart pot. Stir to blend, and cook over medium heat, stirring constantly, for 2 or 3 minutes. Continue stirring, slowly add the milk, and cook for 3 or 4 minutes—the sauce will thicken slightly. Add the rice with its liquid, the lemon juice, nutmeg, and remaining ½ teaspoon salt. Stir to blend, taste for seasoning, and correct if needed. Cook, stirring often, for about 5 minutes. The sauce will thicken more after the addition of the rice and water. Stir in the lemon zest just before serving and serve hot.

Spanish Riso

(five servings)

Riso is the name given to the tiny cut of pasta that resembles grains of rice (*riso* means rice in Italian). There are several kinds of pasta of similar size and shape, including orzo (barley in Italian) and *seme di melone* (melon seeds); you can use them interchangeably.

1½ cups *riso* pasta
6 tablespoons olive oil
8 medium tomatoes, chopped
  (about 4 cups)
2 green bell peppers, seeded,
  deveined, and chopped into
  small dice (about 1½ cups)

½ cup chopped scallions
4 cloves garlic, finely chopped
Salt and pepper to taste
4 tablespoons chopped fresh
  basil
½ teaspoon Tabasco sauce

Bring a large pot of salted water to a boil. Add the *riso*, stir, and boil until the pasta is tender, about 10 minutes. Drain and set aside.

While the *riso* is cooking, put 3 tablespoons of the olive oil in a large sauté pan over medium heat. Add the tomatoes, bell peppers, scallions, and garlic. Cook the tomato mixture about 10 minutes, stirring often. Remove from the heat and stir in the cooked *riso*. Use a whisk to stir if the *riso* is in clumps. When the *riso* is separated, add salt and pepper, and stir in the fresh basil, Tabasco sauce, and the remaining 3 tablespoons of olive oil. Reheat if necessary and serve hot. This will keep several days in the refrigerator.

Marietta's Spaghetti

(four servings)

Marietta is the Italian daughter-in-law of my very old friend Comfort Scott, and this is her suppertime claim to fame. Tomato sauce made in this utterly simple way is quite delicious, and it has an appealing mixture of textures and flavors.

12 Roma or plum tomatoes
  (1¾ pounds), cut in half lengthwise
Salt and pepper to taste
3 cloves garlic, finely chopped
½ cup chopped parsley

½ cup olive oil
1 pound dried spaghetti
2 tablespoons butter, melted
½ cup fresh basil, torn into
  small pieces

Preheat the oven to 350°F.

Put the tomatoes, cut side up, in a 9 × 13-inch baking dish. Salt and pepper them lightly.

Mix together the garlic, ⅓ cup of the parsley, and 2 tablespoons of the olive oil in a small bowl. Pat the garlic mixture on the tomatoes and drizzle 2 more tablespoons of the olive oil over all. Bake, uncovered, for about 45 to 55 minutes, or until the tomatoes are mushy.

About 20 minutes before the tomatoes are done, put a large pot of salted water on for the spaghetti. When the water is boiling, add the spaghetti, stir, and after about 12 minutes, start testing every minute or so until the spaghetti is tender, but firm. Drain.

Mix together the remaining parsley and olive oil, the butter, and the basil in a large bowl. Add the tomatoes and spaghetti. Toss to mix well, and serve.

Iceberg Lettuce and Noodles

(six servings)

This is an exciting dish. It is the kind of recipe I like: a few plain ingredients; a little measuring, cooking, stirring, and tossing— briefly, in one pot; and a wholesome, unusual dish is brought forth. (It is *not* a cold pasta salad. One of the best things about this dish is the contrast between the cold crisp lettuce and the soft hot noodles.)

5 cups chopped iceberg lettuce (in large bite-size pieces)	4 medium zucchini, chopped into bite-size pieces (3 cups)
2 or 3 medium tomatoes, chopped, at room temperature	Optional: 2 cloves garlic, minced
Salt and pepper to taste	6 tablespoons olive oil
8 ounces dried egg noodles, ⅛ to ¼ inch wide	1½ ounces Parmesan cheese, freshly grated (½ cup)

Bring 4 quarts of water to a boil. Meanwhile, put the lettuce and tomatoes in the bottom of a 4- or 5-quart serving or mixing bowl, and lightly salt and pepper. Set aside.

Put the noodles into the boiling water and cook for about 5 minutes. Add the zucchini and cook until the noodles and the zucchini are tender, about 3 more minutes. Drain and heap on top of the lettuce mixture. If using the optional garlic, add it now, salt and pepper the noodles, and pour the olive oil on top. With your hands, quickly and lightly toss and mix. Sprinkle the cheese over and serve, or fill individual bowls and sprinkle the cheese evenly over each serving. Do the last mixing quickly and serve at once.

Pasta Shells, Mushrooms, and Brown Butter

(three or four servings)

This is a winter supper dish. The pasta shells are rich and filling, suffused with the flavors of beef broth, mushrooms, and nutlike browned butter. Crisp, toasted bread crumbs finish the dish perfectly.

½ pound large pasta shells
1 cup beef broth
½ pound fresh mushrooms,
   wiped clean and sliced
   (4 cups)

1 cup white bread crumbs
4 tablespoons (½ stick) butter
Salt and freshly ground
   pepper to taste

Bring a large pot of salted water to a boil. Stir in the pasta shells and cook 20 to 25 minutes, stirring occasionally, so they don't stick to the bottom of the pot. They should be tender, not undercooked.

Meanwhile, heat ½ cup of the beef broth in a large sauté pan. Add the mushrooms and cook over low heat, stirring constantly, until they darken a little and soften, about 3 to 5 minutes. Remove them to a large serving bowl and set aside.

Preheat the oven to 350°F.

Spread the bread crumbs on a cookie sheet and toast them, checking them often because they can burn in a minute or two. Stir so they get evenly toasted. When they are golden, remove and set aside; turn off the oven.

Place the mushrooms with their broth and the remaining ½ cup beef broth in a bowl. Add the cooked, drained pasta shells to the bowl. Place the bowl in the still-warm oven.

Heat the butter in a small saucepan over medium-high heat. It will foam up, subside, then quickly begin to brown. Watch carefully and as soon as it is nut brown, remove from the heat. Stir the browned butter into the pasta, tossing to coat all the shells. Taste and add salt and pepper as needed. Sprinkle the crumbs over the top and serve.

Macaroni and Cheese

(three servings)

A good macaroni and cheese dish should be moist and creamy, with a little bit of chewiness, and a noticeable cheese taste. You get it all with this dish. The recipe can easily be doubled.

1 cup dried elbow macaroni	2 tablespoons flour
Optional: 1 cup buttered bread crumbs to sprinkle over the top	1½ cups milk
	Salt to taste
2 tablespoons butter	3 ounces sharp Cheddar cheese, grated (about 1 cup)

Bring a pot of salted water to a boil and add the macaroni, stirring once or twice while cooking. Cook about 7 minutes, or until just tender, and drain, leaving a little water in the bottom of the pot. Toss the macaroni in the pot and loosely cover until the cheese sauce is made.

Preheat the oven to 350°F. Butter a 1-quart casserole. If using the optional bread crumbs, make them now: lightly brown the bread crumbs in a skillet with butter over medium-high heat; 1 tablespoon of butter is enough for 1 cup of crumbs.

Melt the 2 tablespoons butter in a sauté pan, add the flour, and stir constantly, cooking the *roux* (flour and butter) for about 2 minutes. Slowly add the milk, stirring constantly, add salt to taste, and continue to cook over medium heat, stirring until the sauce is thickened. Remove from the heat and stir in the grated cheese until it has melted and is smoothly blended. Pour the sauce over the macaroni and toss and mix well. Put the pasta and sauce into the casserole, sprinkle the bread crumbs over the top, if desired, and bake for about 30 minutes, or until lightly golden on top. Don't overbake or the macaroni will dry out.

Curried Macaroni

(six servings)

A pleasing dish that looks Indian to me, with its dramatic colors of orange curry and bright green cilantro. Accompany this with dark bread and a mild, white cheese, and Wirtabel's Melon Chutney (see page 178).

2 cups dried elbow macaroni	4 teaspoons curry powder
2 tablespoons butter	Salt and pepper to taste
2 tablespoons flour	½ cup cilantro leaves
2 cups milk	

In a large pot, bring 6 quarts of salted water to a boil. Add the macaroni and cook until it is just barely soft, about 10 minutes. Drain the macaroni and put it in a bowl.

Melt the butter in a medium-size saucepan over medium heat. Add the flour, stirring constantly until thoroughly blended. Slowly add the milk and continue to stir while the sauce cooks. Stir until it is thickened, about 2 or 3 minutes. Add the curry powder and salt and pepper to taste. Pour the sauce over the macaroni and mix together. Stir in the cilantro leaves and serve.

Custard Sandwich

(four servings)

This dish can't fail as long as it sits at least six hours before you bake it. Prepare it the night before or in the morning. It will puff and turn golden brown on top while baking. It is a rich custard, delicate but filling. Serve with small plates of salad and Pineapple Blizzard (see page 227) for dessert.

6 slices bread, buttered
Salt and pepper to taste
4½ ounces sharp Cheddar,
   Gouda, Provolone, Monterey
   Jack, or any other melting
   cheese, grated (1½ cups)

1½ cups milk
6 eggs, slightly beaten

Arrange the slices of bread in a single layer in a shallow, buttered baking dish. Sprinkle lightly with salt and pepper. Sprinkle the grated cheese evenly over the bread. Put the milk and eggs in a bowl, and stir until blended. Pour the milk mixture over the bread and cheese. Cover and refrigerate at least 6 hours, or overnight.

As the dish will be chilled when you are ready to bake it, start it in a cold oven, then immediately turn the heat on to 350°F. Bake for about 1 hour, or until the bread custard is puffy and lightly golden.

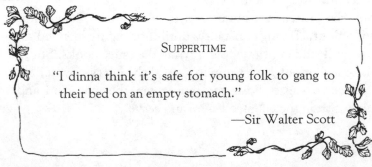

SUPPERTIME

"I dinna think it's safe for young folk to gang to their bed on an empty stomach."

—Sir Walter Scott

Frieda and Elinor's Onion Pie

(eight to ten servings)

If you are ever entertaining a concert artist after a recital, this is your recipe! Elinor got it from a Swiss friend, Frieda, and served it at late-night suppers for community concert guests who played in her Idaho town. This pie is just an onion quiche by another name, transformed by the flavor of tiny caraway seeds.

4 tablespoons (½ stick) butter
8 medium onions, thinly sliced
   and lightly salted
3 eggs
½ cup flour
1 teaspoon salt
½ teaspoon freshly ground
   pepper

1 teaspoon caraway seeds
2 cups half-and-half (half milk
   and half cream)
10-inch pie shell, prebaked 10
   minutes

Preheat the oven to 350°F.

Melt the butter in a large skillet, add the onions, and cook over medium heat for about 15 minutes, or until quite brown. In a large bowl, lightly beat the eggs, then add the flour, salt, pepper, caraway seeds, and half-and-half, and mix well. Mix in the onions, and pour the mixture into the pie shell. Bake for 35 to 45 minutes, or until the pie is just set. Serve warm or cold.

Papusas

(six papusas)

In El Salvador, vendors everywhere sell a street food called *papusas*. They look like slightly thick tortillas, about three inches in diameter. Hidden inside is a filling—either of cheese, as in this recipe, or spicy meat. They are always served with a finely chopped, vinegary coleslaw with fiery pepper and sometimes cilantro (see L.A. Slaw, page 188).

2 cups masa harina (see Note, page 37)
1½ cups warm water
1 tablespoon ground cumin, made from lightly toasted cumin seeds (*comino* in Spanish)

Salt and pepper to taste
6 ounces Ranchero cheese, or mild melting cheese such as Monterey Jack, grated (2 cups)
½ cup chopped cilantro

In a mixing bowl, mix together the masa harina, water, cumin, and ½ teaspoon salt and stir into a manageable dough. The dough should be soft but not sticky; add more flour if needed. If dough is dry and hard to form, add more water. To make 3-inch round *papusas*, put about ½ cup of the dough in your hand for each *papusa*. Roll into a ball and flatten in your hand. Put ⅓ cup cheese, 1 teaspoon cilantro, and salt and pepper to taste in the center. Work the edges up over the filling and again form a ball, completely enclosing the filling. This takes only a few seconds. Flatten each ball to about ¼ inch or less and cook the *papusas* on a hot, lightly oiled griddle for about 3 minutes per side, or until both sides are lightly browned. Serve warm.

Green Chile Pie

(one 9-inch pie)

This is a recipe that makes one of the best all-around supper dishes I can think of. Instead of a pastry crust, the chilis form the shell holding the filling. It is fast to make, and it fits anywhere, anytime.

6 or 7 California or Anaheim chile peppers (see Note and roasting instructions, page 113), peeled, split, and seeded; or about 10 ounces canned roasted whole green chile peppers
3½ ounces fontina or any mild soft white cheese, grated (1¼ cups)

4 eggs
2 cups light cream (or 1½ cups milk)
½ teaspoon salt
Pepper to taste
¼ cup whole cilantro leaves, stems removed

Preheat the oven to 425°F.

Butter the bottom of a 9-inch pie pan. Line the buttered pie pan with the split chiles, insides up, so that they cover the bottom and sides of the pan. Sprinkle the cheese evenly over the chiles.

Break the eggs into a bowl and lightly beat with a whisk until they are broken and blended. Add the cream and the salt and pepper. Mix well. Pour the custard over the cheese.

Bake for 15 minutes at 425°F, then lower the heat to 325°F. Bake for 20 to 30 minutes more, or until the custard seems set. If the center trembles a bit, remove from the oven (the custard continues to cook a little). Don't overcook: a knife inserted halfway from the center should come out clean when the pie is done. Put lots of cilantro on top. Serve hot or cold with warm tortillas (see page 113).

Potato and Pepper Frittata

(four servings)

I'm not crazy about frittatas because they often taste too much like overcooked cold eggs. This one is different. All its flavors come together somehow without that excessive eggy taste. And it looks pretty, with bright green strips of pepper embedded in its crisp golden top.

4 tablespoons olive oil
1 medium potato, peeled, quartered, and sliced ¼ inch thick
1 green bell pepper, seeded, deveined, and sliced in strips

1 medium onion, halved and sliced
1 clove garlic, finely chopped
6 eggs
Salt and pepper to taste

In a 10- to 12-inch skillet, put 2 tablespoons of the olive oil. Add the potato and cook over medium heat until it is tender and browned, about 10 to 15 minutes. Remove to a plate and set aside.

Put the remaining olive oil in the skillet over medium heat, add the pepper and onion and cook until soft, about 10 minutes. Stir in the potato and garlic. Put the eggs in a bowl and beat lightly, just until yolks and whites are blended. Add salt and pepper and pour over the vegetable mixture. Reduce the heat to low, cover the skillet, and cook for 8 to 10 minutes, or until the top looks set. Check the frittata after about 7 minutes—overcooking will make the eggs too dry. Cut the frittata into wedges and serve right away with the golden bottom side up.

Tomato Rarebit

(four servings)

Tomato Rarebit is a simple, old-fashioned one-pan supper dish.
Serve with some extra toast and Tiny Herb Salads (see page 190).

2 medium tomatoes, finely chopped	2 eggs, slightly beaten
¼ teaspoon baking soda	1 teaspoon dry mustard
2 tablespoons butter	¼ to ½ teaspoon cayenne
2 tablespoons flour	pepper
1 cup milk, heated	Salt to taste
5 ounces Cheddar cheese,	8 slices toast
grated (1½ cups)	

Mix together the chopped tomatoes and the baking soda and set
aside. Melt the butter in a saucepan, stir in the flour, and cook for
about 2 to 3 minutes, stirring constantly. Slowly pour in the heated
milk and stir until the mixture is smooth and thick.

Add the tomatoes, cheese, eggs, mustard, cayenne pepper, and
salt. Cook over very low heat, stirring until the cheese melts and
the mixture is smooth and well blended. Serve hot over the toast.

HAVING SUPPER OUT

"I went into the Parker House one night about midnight, and I
saw four doctors there eating lobster salad, and deviled crab, and
washing it down with champagne, and I made up my mind that
the doctors needn't talk to me any more about what was wholesome. I was going for what was *good*. And there ain't anything
better for supper than Welsh rabbit in *this* world."

—William Dean Howells, 1882

Linda Sue's Tomato Stew

(four servings)

My friend Linda Sue told me that when she was growing up her Aunt Fanny Scott would make her this tomato stew whenever Linda Sue was feeling blue.

3 slices smoky-style bacon, diced
1 red onion, chopped
4 cups stewed tomatoes; or about 8 fresh tomatoes, chopped
1 teaspoon sugar
Salt and pepper to taste
½ teaspoon Tabasco sauce, or to taste
4 or 5 biscuits, broken into large pieces; or 4 slices bread, torn into large pieces

Heat a Dutch oven, or other heavy-bottomed pot, and add the bacon and onion. Cook over medium-low heat, stirring often, until the onion is soft and the bacon is slightly browned. Add the tomatoes, sugar, salt and pepper, and Tabasco. Cook for 10 minutes, stirring often. Add the broken biscuits and cook 2 or 3 minutes more. Serve hot, but this is good served cold, too.

Bread and Bacon Pancake

(one thin 10-inch pancake, or four servings)

This makes a crunchy pancake with a robust smoky taste. It would be good with strong-flavored green vegetables such as spinach with garlic, mustard greens, or curly endive or chicory in garlic vinaigrette.

6 slices white bread, cut into ½-inch cubes (6 cups in all)
4 teaspoons cider vinegar
1 cup water

4 slices smoky-style bacon, cut into small dice
Salt and pepper to taste

Put the bread cubes in a bowl. Mix the vinegar with the water and sprinkle evenly over the bread cubes. Gently toss to mix well. Let the cubes stand a couple of hours.

Put the diced bacon in a 10-inch skillet. Cook a minute or two over medium-low heat, stirring often (you should have about ¼ cup fat; if not, add 1 tablespoon or so of vegetable oil). Sprinkle the bread cubes on top of the bacon. Using a spatula, press the bread cubes down, and salt and pepper liberally. Turn the heat to simmer and let the pancake slowly brown and crisp on the bottom. After 10 to 15 minutes, gently lift the edge of the pancake with the spatula to see that it is not cooking too rapidly and burning.

When the pancake is a deep golden color, cut down the center and turn over each half. Continue to cook until the other side is crisp and golden. Remove to a platter, cut to make 4 wedges, and serve hot.

EXPATRIATE SUPPERS

"When in 1908 I went to live with Gertrude Stein at the rue de Fleurus she said we would have American food for Sunday-evening supper, she had had enough of French and Italian cooking . . . So I commenced to cook the simple dishes I had eaten in the homes of the San Joaquin Valley in California—fricasseed chicken, corn bread, apple and lemon pie . . . "

—from *The Alice B. Toklas Cookbook*

Supper Breads

Hamburger Buns

Rye Crackers

Lemon Crackers

Lil's Ice-Water Crackers

Garlic Rolls

Popovers

Crusty Popovers

Sharp Cheddar Biscuits

Brown Bread Muffins

Buttermilk Cornbread

Irish Soda Bread

Date-Nut Bread

Gingerbread or Gingercake

You may be a born-to-bake person who has never given it a try. Anyone can bake good things at home. Baking is a different experience from cooking. Stir a few mundane ingredients together, pop the batter or dough into the oven, and as if by sleight of hand, what went into the oven is transformed into something golden, lofty, and usually delicious.

To be confident when you begin baking, you need to have good recipes. Recipes vary a lot, and some produce better results than others. The best way to get a good baking book is to ask a friend who bakes a lot, or the local food editor on your newspaper, or someone in town who runs a cooking school. Also buy an inexpensive oven thermometer and double-check the temperature of your oven. Always use a kitchen timer when baking: it is very easy to become distracted at home and let baking things burn.

The recipes in this chapter are mostly for breads you can't buy in stores, including some things one doesn't generally think of as breads. For example, there are great Popovers, an almost forgotten supper treat (see page 150); homemade Rye Crackers (see page 145); and Gingerbread with a split personality—it can be a bread with roasted spareribs, or a cake (see page 158). And there are recipes to transform the bread you *do* buy in stores: the amazing Lil's Ice-

Water Crackers (see page 148) and magic Garlic Rolls (see page 149)—the danger with these is that people will devour them and forget to eat anything else!

Hamburger Buns

(makes sixteen 3½-inch buns)

This recipe makes the world's best hamburger buns—they stay together so fillings aren't falling all over the place, and yet they are moist and tender. Wrapped carefully, these freeze well. Use them within two months.

1½ cups warm water	3 tablespoons sugar
⅔ cup instant nonfat dry milk	2 packages dry yeast
⅓ cup lard or vegetable shortening	1 egg
1½ teaspoons salt	About 5½ cups all-purpose flour

Put the water, dry milk, lard, salt, and sugar in a mixing bowl and stir to blend. Sprinkle the yeast over the mixture, stir, then let stand to dissolve for a couple of minutes. Add the egg and 2 cups of the flour. Beat vigorously until thoroughly blended and smooth. Add enough of the remaining flour to make a manageable dough. Turn out onto a lightly floured surface and knead for a minute. Let rest for 10 minutes.

Add enough additional flour so that the dough is not sticky, and resume kneading until smooth and elastic. Place the dough in a large greased bowl, cover, and let rise until it is double in bulk.

Grease some baking sheets. Punch the dough down and divide in half, then cut each half into 8 equal pieces. Roll each piece between your palms into a smooth ball and place about 3 inches apart on the baking sheets. Pressing down with the palm of your hand, flatten each ball into a circle about 3 inches in diameter. Cover lightly and let rise for about 45 minutes, or until double in bulk.

Preheat the oven to 425°F.

Bake the buns for 20 to 25 minutes, or until lightly browned. Remove from the baking sheets and cool on racks.

Rye Crackers

(about forty 2½-inch squares)

Homemade rye crackers are so much better than the store-bought variety. They're coarser and crunchier, with a hardy, rustic taste. Nothing could be simpler to make, and, stored in an airtight container, they keep almost indefinitely.

1½ cups all-purpose flour
½ cup rye flour
½ teaspoon salt
2 tablespoons cold butter

⅔ cup milk, plus a bit more if needed
2 teaspoons kosher salt

Preheat the oven to 425°F.

Put the flours and salt in a large mixing bowl and stir to blend with a fork. Cut the butter into small bits and add to the flour mixture. Use your fingertips or a pastry blender to rub or cut the butter into the flour. The mixture should look like coarse meal. Slowly add the milk, stirring with a fork, until the dough forms a rough ball and pulls away from the side of the bowl. If the dough seems dry, add a few drops more milk; it should be soft and pliable, not wet and sticky.

Divide the dough in half and shape each piece into a rough

square with your hands. Lightly dust a board with flour and roll out the first piece into about a 14-inch square—the thickness should be less than ½ inch. Trim the edges so they are neat. Roll the dough up on the rolling pin and unroll onto an ungreased baking sheet. Use a sharp knife to score the dough into 2½-inch squares, cutting almost through so the finished crackers will break apart in neat squares. With a fork, prick each square in 3 places. Sprinkle 1 teaspoon of the kosher salt evenly over the dough. Bake for 5 or 6 minutes, or until the edges are nicely browned. Slide off the baking sheet and cool. Break apart.

Meanwhile, roll out the remaining rough square of dough, following the directions above, and bake. Store the crackers in an airtight container.

Lemon Crackers

(seventy-two 2-inch square crackers)

Before I'd ever seen—let alone tasted—a lemon cracker, I felt the need for one. These go well with many things: salads, vegetable soups, and fish dishes such as Fillet of Sole with Fresh Bread Crumbs (see page 53) or Cioppino (see page 44).

2 cups all-purpose flour	4 tablespoons (½ stick)
1½ tablespoons sugar	butter
½ teaspoon salt	⅔ cup milk, plus a few
3 tablespoons finely grated	drops more if needed
lemon peel	1 tablespoon kosher salt

Preheat the oven to 325°F.

In a large mixing bowl, mix together the flour, sugar, salt, and 1½ tablespoons of the lemon peel. With a pastry blender, cut in the butter until the mixture resembles fine crumbs. With a fork, mix the milk into the flour mixture until a ball of dough is formed. If there are a few dry crumbs, add a little more milk, a few drops at a time, until all of the dough is moistened.

Divide the dough in half. On a lightly floured board, form half of the dough into a 4-inch square. Roll into a 12-inch square, making sure to flour the board and rolling pin as needed to prevent sticking. The finished dough should be very thin, no more than $\frac{1}{8}$ inch thick. Transfer the dough to an ungreased cookie sheet by placing the sheet alongside the dough, then gently lifting the dough onto the sheet. With a knife, score the dough into 2-inch squares, then with a fork prick each dough square in 3 places, poking all the way through to the cookie sheet. Mix together the kosher salt and remaining lemon peel. Sprinkle half of this lemon salt over the square and press lightly into the dough. Bake for 15 minutes, or until an even golden brown. Remove from the oven and turn the cracker over. Return to the oven and bake for an additional 5 to 6 minutes, or until lightly golden brown on the second side. When the cracker is done, remove from the oven and gently break into pieces along the scored lines.

Repeat the procedure with the remaining dough. Cool the crackers completely and store in an airtight container.

Lil's Ice-Water Crackers

(two dozen crackers)

This unlikely recipe was given to me a long time ago in Los Angeles. It turns ordinary saltines into crunchy, buttery crackers. They
are worth the little trouble they take and eating one invites you to
eat a hundred. Try Lil's Ice-Water Crackers with Chicken Custard
in Broth (see page 46) or Joyce McGillis's Creamy Corn Soup (see
page 36).

24 plain saltine crackers	½ cup (1 stick) butter, melted
4 cups ice water	Optional: 1 teaspoon salt

Preheat the oven to 475°F.

Lay the crackers in a single layer in a 10 × 15 × ¾-inch baking
pan. (A pan this size will hold 35 crackers, but use only 24 because
they swell and expand when soaked in ice water.) Pour the ice water
over them and let stand for about 5 minutes. Carefully remove the
crackers with a metal spatula or slotted spoon, or gently remove
with your hands, and place on a double layer of paper towels (laid
over a folded tea towel) to drain for 5 minutes.

Dry the baking pan and pour half the melted butter over the bottom; spread with your fingers. Arrange the crackers on the pan and
drizzle the remaining butter over them. If the crackers aren't very
salty, sprinkle the optional salt over them.

Put in the hot oven and bake for 15 to 20 minutes, or until
lightly golden. Serve immediately. They can be kept in an airtight
container, but they are best just out of the oven.

Garlic Rolls

(eight rolls)

These garlic rolls are a thrill. When you read this recipe you'll think "garlic bread," and feel like you know what Garlic Rolls are all about. You don't. This is a whole different kind of experience. You can even justify your indulgence in these since you'll skip using butter entirely. The Italians take credit for this invention, and so do the Ukrainians.

½ teaspoon kosher salt
1 tablespoon water
1 teaspoon finely chopped
   garlic
2 teaspoons finely chopped
   parsley

¼ cup vegetable oil
8 heated soft, white dinner
   rolls, American homemade-
   type, like Parker House or
   cloverleaf

In a small bowl, stir the salt into the water and let stand for 5 minutes until the salt is dissolved; then stir again. Add the garlic, parsley, and oil and mix well. Put the heated rolls close together in a shallow dish and drizzle the flavored oil evenly over them. Serve immediately.

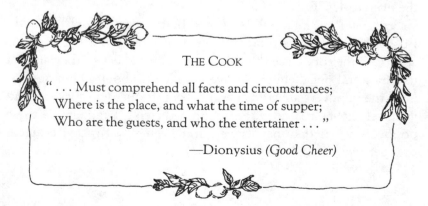

THE COOK

" ... Must comprehend all facts and circumstances;
Where is the place, and what the time of supper;
Who are the guests, and who the entertainer ... "

—Dionysius *(Good Cheer)*

Popovers

(about seven popovers)

The glory of popovers is their incredible size, crusty outsides, and creamy, tender, and almost hollow insides just waiting for butter and a spoonful of strawberry jam. But I had about given up on making them over the last few years because they kept turning out to be sullen little muffins, pop-unders. I had forgotten that popovers rise highest when they get a forceful amount of heat quickly, and I had been using muffin tins instead of separate containers like ovenproof Pyrex glass baking cups, which work perfectly. I had a thrill when I opened the oven door and my popovers were once again giant golden balloons. Popovers are meant to go with chicken, roasts, salads, and soups; they don't belong with spaghetti, curries, or chili. For perfect popovers, see the popover principles at the end of the recipe.

1½ cups all-purpose flour	3 eggs
1½ cups milk	3 tablespoons butter, melted
1 teaspoon salt	

Grease Pyrex glass ¾-cup-size cups (I use butter or Pam). Preheat the oven to 425°F.

Beat the flour, milk, salt, eggs, and butter together until smooth. I use a blender, but a rotary beater works fine, too. Fill the cups almost to the top. Place the cups on a baking sheet so they are not touching and put them in the oven. Bake for about 30 minutes, or until the popovers are golden and light. Lift one out of its cup and if it feels light, it is done. Serve immediately. (I rather like these popovers when they have fallen and been rewarmed. Reheated, they get some of their puffiness back.)

POPOVER PRINCIPLES

1. Individual baking cups, such as Pyrex, work the best.

2. Fill the cups almost to the top with batter.

3. Always bake popovers in the bottom third of the oven.

4. Spear the popovers with a very sharp knife to release the steam from inside right after they are taken out of the oven.

5. Serve them immediately from the oven as popovers do fall slowly as they cool.

Crusty Popovers

(twelve popovers)

A little sleight of hand in the kitchen: remarkable that this cream puff dough gives results so similar to popover batter. However, these Crusty Popovers are guaranteed to hold their shape and not collapse. They can do double duty, either as popovers with savory foods or as cream puff shells for dessert fillings. Be sure they bake long enough; their hollow centers won't be creamy like the insides of popovers. Serve immediately.

1 cup water
½ cup (1 stick) butter
1 cup all-purpose flour

1 teaspoon salt
5 eggs

Preheat the oven to 400°F.

In a medium-size saucepan, bring the water and butter to a boil over medium-high heat. When the butter is melted and the mixture is boiling, add the flour all at once and briskly stir until the mixture forms a ball and pulls away from the side of the pan. Cook, stirring, about 2 to 3 minutes. Remove the pan from the heat and let cool for about 5 minutes, stirring occasionally. The temperature should be 140°F. Add the eggs, one at a time, briskly beating until each egg is completely blended into the dough. Grease twelve ¾-cup Pyrex dishes and place a mound of the dough the size of a golf ball in each dish. Place the dishes on a cookie sheet and bake for 35 minutes, or until the popovers are deep golden and sound hollow when tapped. Remove from the cups and serve immediately, unless you are filling them to serve as dessert.

Sharp Cheddar Biscuits

(sixteen biscuits)

Little savory cheese biscuits flecked with Cheddar, fresh and warm from the oven, are just what you need with some of the cold supper salads in this book like Green Rose Salad (see page 10), and Waldorf Salad (see page 14). Certainly they are the right biscuit with Mustard Green Soup (see page 30).

2 cups all-purpose flour
½ teaspoon salt
4 teaspoons baking powder
1 tablespoon sugar
3 ounces sharp Cheddar
  cheese, grated (1 cup)

½ cup vegetable shortening,
  chilled
⅔ cup milk

Preheat the oven to 425°F.

In a mixing bowl, mix together the flour, salt, baking powder, sugar, and cheese. Using a pastry blender or two knives, cut the vegetable shortening into the flour mixture until it resembles coarse meal. Add the milk all at once and stir with a fork until the dry ingredients are moistened.

Turn the dough out on a lightly floured board and knead 10 times. Pat the dough until it is ½ inch thick and cut into rounds, using a 2-inch cutter. Pat the scraps into a square and recut. Arrange the rounds on an ungreased cookie sheet so that the edges of the rounds touch. Bake 15 to 20 minutes, or until the tops are lightly browned. Serve immediately.

Brown Bread Muffins

(eighteen muffins)

The combination of cornmeal, two kinds of flour, and raisins makes brown bread muffins moist, flavorful, and nutritious. They are accommodating to lots of different foods—the New England tradition is to eat them with Boston Baked Beans (see page 111)—or try them with Ham and Bean Soup (see page 27) or Tri-Tip Pot Roast (see page 91). For an early spring supper, serve Asparagus Salad (see page 12) and soft white cheese with them.

1 cup all-purpose flour	¾ cup dark molasses
1 cup whole wheat flour	4 tablespoons cider vinegar
1 cup yellow cornmeal	1¼ cups milk
1½ teaspoons baking soda	2 tablespoons butter, melted
1½ teaspoons salt	1 cup raisins

Preheat the oven to 400°F. Grease 18 muffin tins.

Put the all-purpose flour, whole wheat flour, yellow cornmeal, baking soda, and salt in a large mixing bowl. Stir the dry ingredients with a fork to mix and blend well. Add the molasses, vinegar, milk, and butter, and stir briskly to blend. Stir in the raisins. Fill the muffin tins three-quarters full with the batter.

Bake for about 12 minutes, or until a straw inserted into the center of a muffin comes out clean. Remove from the oven and serve warm. These freeze well.

TAKING SUPPER TO THE SICK OR BEREAVED

The old custom of taking homemade food to a sick friend or a bereaved family is almost forgotten today. Sympathy or get-well cards, flowers, and house plants have replaced chicken noodle soup. Cards and flowers are consoling, but food is the best gift of all. When there has been a death in the family the last thing anyone cares to think about is food, but when friends and relatives arrive to pay their respects, being able to offer some cold sliced ham and a salad or a plate of cookies and a cup of coffee or tea gives one the feeling that life can go on as usual.

The most appropriate food to take to a bereaved family is good, plain food that keeps well and requires little fuss to serve. I think it is hard to beat a baked ham, the makings of a salad, a loaf of homemade bread, some Applesauce (see page 179), and Parker Brownies (see page 211).

When visiting a sick friend, my old standbys are Rich Chicken Noodle Soup (see page 47) and Baked Vanilla Custard (see page 223). Chicken noodle soup has well-known curative powers, and plain custards almost always seem nourishing and digestible, even to someone who is very ill.

Buttermilk Cornbread

(six servings)

There are many types of cornbread. This one is fine textured and slightly buttermilk sour, with a very thin layer of custard formed by the milk poured over it just before it's baked.

2 tablespoons butter	1 teaspoon baking soda
½ cup all-purpose flour	2 eggs
1¼ cups yellow cornmeal	2 cups buttermilk
1 teaspoon salt	1½ cups milk

Preheat the oven to 350°F.

Put the butter in a 8 × 8 × 2-inch square baking dish. Put the dish in the oven and let the butter melt. Remove the dish from the oven and tilt the dish so the butter coats the sides and bottom.

Sift the flour, cornmeal, salt, and baking soda into a mixing bowl. Beat the eggs until they have a little foam on top, and add to the dry ingredients. Add the buttermilk and 1 cup of the milk, and stir briskly until well blended.

Pour the batter into the baking dish and, without stirring, pour the remaining ½ cup of milk in the center of the batter. This will create a thin white layer of custard. Bake for about 40 to 50 minutes, or until a straw comes out clean when inserted in the center. Serve warm.

Irish Soda Bread

(one 9-inch round loaf)

With Irish Soda Bread you don't have to wait around for risings and proofings—you just stir it up and put it in the oven. When it comes out it looks as if it just arrived from the Irish countryside: rustic and homey, brown whole wheat flecked with creamy-colored oats. In theory you should wait for it to cool before you slice it, but I always weaken and slice it while it's warm, even though it crumbles.

2½ cups milk	½ cup rolled oats
2 tablespoons white vinegar	1 teaspoon baking soda
4 cups whole wheat flour	2 teaspoons salt
1 cup all-purpose white flour	

Preheat the oven to 375°F.

Put the milk in a small bowl. Stir in the vinegar and mix to make the milk sour; set aside. In a large mixing bowl, mix together the whole wheat flour, white flour, oats, baking soda, and salt. Add the soured milk to the flour mixture and stir until all the dry ingredients are moistened. Place the dough on a floured board and lightly knead about 10 times, until the dough is smooth.

Form the dough into a 9-inch round loaf, place it on a cookie sheet, and with a sharp knife, mark the top of the loaf with an X, cutting into the dough about ⅛ inch deep. Bake for 50 to 60 minutes, or until the bread is brown and sounds hollow when tapped. Cool and serve.

Date-Nut Bread

(one 8½ × 4½ × 3-inch loaf)

This is the best-tasting of all the date-nut breads, and I've made a lot of them. It has good texture, it's more moist, it's more flavorful, and the balance of sweetness is just right. Date-nut bread used to be the most popular of the sweet breads, or tea breads. Sliced very thin and spread with cream cheese or sweet butter, it was served in all the tearooms. The recipe came to me from Mary Jo Thompson, who used to own and run a little country inn in Fiddletown, California.

1 cup coarsely chopped pitted dates	1 cup granulated sugar
1½ teaspoons baking soda	1½ cups all-purpose flour
3 tablespoons butter	½ teaspoon salt
¾ cup boiling water	1 teaspoon vanilla
2 eggs	1 cup coarsely chopped walnuts

Lightly mix together the dates and the baking soda, and add the butter. Mix in the boiling water, and let stand for 20 minutes.

Preheat the oven to 325°F. Butter the loaf pan.

In another bowl, beat the eggs lightly with a fork, and add the sugar, flour, salt, and vanilla, and mix well. Add the walnuts and then the date mixture and stir until just blended. Pour into the buttered loaf pan and bake for 40 to 50 minutes; the bread is done when a toothpick comes out clean. Be careful not to overbake. Let cool and spread thin slices with cream cheese.

Gingerbread or Gingercake

(six servings)

Years ago gingerbread was often served as bread with supper, and I wish this old custom could be revived. Ham and Bean Soup (see page 27) and gingerbread make a great combination, and you've missed something if you've never had Black Pepper Ribs (see page 102) with gingerbread hot from the oven. For a light supper, serve warm gingerbread with Applesauce (see page 179) and sharp Cheddar cheese, as the English do; for a lively one, try gingerbread with curried dishes such as kedgeree or Laguna Beach Shrimp Curry (see page 58). With four more tablespoons of sugar added, the flavors are more dessertlike, and the gingerbread becomes Gingercake.

½ cup (1 stick) butter, room temperature	½ teaspoon salt
	1 teaspoon baking soda
¾ cup sugar	1 tablespoon ground ginger
1 egg	1 teaspoon cinnamon
½ cup molasses	½ teaspoon ground cloves
2 cups all-purpose flour	1 cup boiling water

Preheat the oven to 350°F. Butter and lightly flour a 7 × 11-inch baking dish.

Put the butter and sugar in a mixing bowl and beat until creamy and blended. Add the egg and molasses and mix well. Add the flour, salt, baking soda, ginger, cinnamon, and cloves, and beat until well blended. Stir in the boiling water and quickly pour into the baking dish. Bake for 35 to 40 minutes, or until a toothpick comes out clean when inserted in the center of the cake, or the sides of the cake shrink a little around the edge of the baking dish. Serve warm.

Fringe Dishes

Sauces, Salsas, and Spreads

Tartar Sauce

Green Sauce

Red Salsa

Apple Butter

Swiss Cheese Spread

Beet Marmalade

Port Wine Jelly

Pickles and Relishes

Pike's Perfect Pickles

Pickled Peppers

Chow Chow

Real Relish

Corn Relish

Fire and Ice Relish

Rhubarb-Onion Relish

Piccalilli

Wirtabel's Melon Chutney

Side Dishes, Slaws, and Small Salads

Applesauce

Fried Apple Rings

Baby Peas and Iceberg Lettuce

Blanche's Cabbage with Bacon

Carrots with Fresh Mint

Cornmeal-Fried Tomatillos

Jasmine Rice

Orzo with Fresh Dill

Deviled Eggs

Coleslaw

L.A. Slaw

Turnip Slaw

Tiny Herb Salads

Crouton Salad

Cucumber Salad

Lettuce in Cream

Wedge of Iceberg with Thick
    Creamy Dressing

Mustard Celery Salad

Relish Salad

Grapefruit, Black Olive, and Mint
    Salad

Persimmon-Pear Salad

F ringe dishes are exciting. Sometimes they are thought to be superfluous, but they are very important. They are the small dishes that surround the main supper dish—condiments, relishes, pickles, preserves, small salads, sauces, and salsas. They are hospitable gifts from the cook which you may choose to eat or ignore. Fringe dishes give you a chance to balance the flavors and texture of your food to suit your taste. Small but mighty, they prove how a little can do a lot: they do what the right jewelry does for an understated dress. Good examples of this would be a spoonful of Beet Marmalade (see page 168) with the Beef Salad with Sour Pickles (see page 22), or the Piccalilli (see page 177) with the American Meatloaf (see page 98). The Jasmine Rice (see page 185) and the Tiny Herb Salads (see page 190) are so brimming with flavor they will bowl you over.

I lament the loss of homemade condiments from the American table. Americans a hundred years ago understood that the niceties of a well-set table included lots more than salt and pepper to entice the appetite. Their tablecloths were almost hidden by small dishes filled with condiments and relishes, and their cellars were generously stacked with quarts of pickles, chow chow, and chutney.

We don't need cellars full of preserves, but a few jars made up in advance and kept on hand in your refrigerator will do wonders for your table. These recipes are for small amounts that are easy to prepare and that keep well when refrigerated.

Tartar Sauce

(one and one-half cups)

Tartar sauce is a lively sauce for fish, presumably named after the marauding nomads of Central Asia—perhaps because it, too, makes a rapid conquest. Tartar sauce is one of those things that people buy out of habit without stopping to think that they can make it in a jiff at home. It is a must on Oyster Buns (see page 64).

1 cup mayonnaise
2 tablespoons finely chopped
  scallions
½ cup finely chopped dill
  pickles

1½ teaspoons chopped capers
½ teaspoon cayenne pepper

In a bowl, put the mayonnaise, scallions, dill pickles, capers, and cayenne and stir until well mixed. Store in the refrigerator in a covered container.

Green Sauce

(about one cup)

This green sauce has a fine sparkle to it that makes it a great all-purpose sauce. Spoon some over cottage cheese, or over new potatoes, or serve it with cold meats. Thinned down with a little more oil, it can be used as a vinaigrette on salads.

½ cup olive oil
2 tablespoons water
1½ tablespoons cider vinegar
½ teaspoon kosher salt
Pepper to taste
1 teaspoon Dijon mustard

2 teaspoons cream-style
   horseradish
2 large cloves garlic
⅓ cup chopped parsley
2 scallions, including tender
   greens, chopped

Put the olive oil, water, vinegar, salt, and pepper in a food processor and process until well blended. Add the mustard, horseradish, garlic, parsley, and scallions and blend well. Store in an airtight jar in the refrigerator until needed.

The old-fashioned way of rounding out flavors at table was to serve relishes and pickles with simple dishes, rather than adding many tastes and textures to a dish.

Red Salsa

(three cups)

Salsas have almost become a kitchen staple over the last several years. This is a moderately hot salsa that has a fresh, balanced flavor. You control the heat of this salsa by the amount of hot sauce or Tabasco you use. The Anaheim pepper is mild. Red Salsa is like a good relish: it can give sparkle to pastas, eggs, or soups (see Sharon's Lentil Salsa Soup, page 31).

6 medium very ripe tomatoes
1 Anaheim pepper (see Note,
    page 113), seeded and deveined
1 large onion
1½ cups loosely packed
    cilantro leaves

3 large cloves garlic, finely
    chopped
5 tablespoons lemon juice
1½ to 2 teaspoons hot sauce,
    such as Tabasco
1 teaspoon salt

Coarsely chop the tomatoes, pepper, onion, and cilantro in a food processor or by hand. Stir in the garlic, lemon juice, hot sauce, and salt. Refrigerate until needed. This keeps a week.

A VISION OF PLENTY

I have a favorite book, *The Country Kitchen*, by Della Lutes, published in 1935, that describes unforgettably the fringe dishes on her family's table at Christmastime in rural Michigan in the late 1800s: "A tumbler of wild grape jelly quivered upturned upon a small glass plate—wild grape because of the muskier tang. Pickled watermelon rind—translucent pink shading to opaque green—drenched in a luscious syrup of citron and lemon flavor reposed on a small dish shaped of two graceful hands . . . of alabaster white." The meal was simple by today's standards, but, she writes: "I have a vision of plenty, appetizingly prepared."

Apple Butter

(six cups)

Apple butter captures the essence of apple—it becomes thick, deeply flavored, and dark from its long, gentle cooking. It is wonderful spread on warm rolls or toast. Use the spices only if your apples are bland.

4 pounds apples, washed,
  cored, and cut into eighths
1½ cups apple cider; or water;
  or a mixture of both
2 tablespoons lemon juice

½ to ⅔ cup sugar, to taste
Optional: 2 teaspoons cinnamon, 1 teaspoon ground
  cloves, and ½ teaspoon
  allspice

Put the apples, liquid, and lemon juice in a large enamel or stainless-steel pot. Bring to a boil, reduce the heat to simmer, and cook until the apples are tender and soft. Remove from the heat and purée until smooth, using either a food mill or a food processor. If your apples are flavorful, use no spice, or very little. If they have the blahs, add the cinnamon, clove, and allspice. Add the sugar and spice at this point and stir to mix well.

Return the puréed apples to the pot and cook over very low heat, stirring often, until the mixture is reduced to about half its volume; this will take about 1½ hours. Test for doneness by placing a spoonful of apple butter on a plate: when it cools there should be no moisture around the rim of the fruit.

To preserve less than a month, spoon into clean jars, cover, and refrigerate when cool. For longer preserving, fill sterilized jars with the hot apple butter, leaving ¼-inch headspace, put on the lids and tighten, and process in a boiling-water canner for 10 minutes.

Swiss Cheese Spread

(two and one-half cups)

Never have I served this without someone saying, "I love it, what's in it? Will you give me the recipe?" Then they are astonished at how simple it is. This recipe makes a pint plus. That is a lot, but it has so many uses: spread it on toast and run under the broiler; or stir a spoonful into your soup—it is quite nice with clear chicken broth.

½ cup mayonnaise
6 ounces Swiss cheese, thinly
  grated (2 cups)

2 tablespoons finely chopped
  parsley

Mix the mayonnaise thoroughly with the Swiss cheese, using enough mayonnaise to make it spreadable. Put in a bowl just large enough to hold it, cover with plastic wrap, and refrigerate. When ready to serve, turn out onto a platter and mold into a mound, using your hands. Sprinkle with the parsley and place crackers around the edge.

Beet Marmalade

(about two cups)

Even those who normally resist beets will like this—their natural sweetness blends perfectly with the flavor of ginger. Serve with Tarragon Fish on Toast (see page 62), Laguna Beach Shrimp Curry (see page 58), or Tri-Tip Pot Roast (see page 91).

4 medium-large beets, cooked and peeled (see page 11)	1 large lemon
1½ cups sugar	2 tablespoons chopped fresh ginger

Put the beets in a food processor and process until coarsely chopped, or mash the beets by hand. Transfer the beets to a heavy-bottomed saucepan and stir in the sugar.

Cut, seed, and quarter the lemon. Put the pieces and the ginger into the food processor and process until finely chopped, or chop by hand. Add the lemon and ginger to the beet mixture and stir to blend. Cook over medium-low heat, stirring often, until the marmalade has thickened a little. This takes about 2 minutes—remember that the marmalade will get even thicker as it cools.

Put the hot marmalade into clean jars, cover, and refrigerate when cool. This will keep for a month. For longer preserving, fill sterilized jars with the hot mixture, leaving ¼-inch headspace. Put on the lids and tighten, and process in a boiling-water canner for 15 minutes.

Port Wine Jelly

(four and one-half cups)

There is something old and complex, musty and mysterious, about the flavors of port wine combined with rosemary that makes chicken or turkey taste better.

2 cups port wine

3 cups sugar

3 tablespoons lemon juice

2 teaspoons chopped fresh
rosemary; or 1½ teaspoons
dried rosemary

½ teaspoon salt

6 ounces liquid pectin

Put the wine, sugar, lemon juice, rosemary, and salt in a saucepan and bring to a boil, stirring until the sugar dissolves. Simmer for 2 minutes, then remove from the heat. Immediately stir in the pectin and strain the jelly into a large measuring cup that will make it easy to pour into four 1-cup jelly glasses. There will be an extra ½ cup left over: put it in a ramekin and use it that evening for supper. I put a sprig of fresh rosemary on top of the jelly when it has set. Cover with a lid and store in the refrigerator. Keeps well for a month.

Pike's Perfect Pickles

(eight cups)

Pike's Perfect Pickles have been a favorite of my old friends, the Edward Pike family, for thirty years. They are like the ideal glass of lemonade, with just enough acid and flavor and just enough sugar.

16 pickling cucumbers, about
    4 to 5 inches, washed and
    thinly sliced
2 medium onions, thinly
    sliced
1 green bell pepper, seeded,
    deveined, and sliced into
    thin strips,
1 sweet red pepper, seeded
    deveined, and sliced into
    thin strips

Salt to taste
4 cups sugar
1½ teaspoons ground tur-
    meric
½ teaspoon ground cloves
1 teaspoon celery seed
1 tablespoon mustard seed
1 quart cider vinegar

Put the sliced cucumbers, onions, and green and red pepper strips in a kettle. Sprinkle lightly with salt and toss so the salt is distributed. Cover the mixture with ice cubes and set aside, covered, for 3 hours.

Drain thoroughly. Stir together in a bowl the sugar, turmeric, cloves, celery seed, mustard seed, and vinegar and mix well. Pour over the cucumber mixture in the kettle. Bring just to a boil, stirring, and immediately remove from the heat.

Spoon the pickles into clean jars, pour the liquid over, and let cool. Cover and refrigerate. These are ready to eat at once. If long preservation is desired, fill sterilized jars with the hot pickles and liquid, leaving a ½-inch headspace at the top of each jar. Put on the lids and tighten, and process in a boiling-water bath for 10 minutes. Remove the jars from the kettle and cool.

Pickled Peppers

(two cups)

Pickled Peppers are a little tart and a little tangy with a roasted pepper taste. They are great with a Swiss cheese sandwich—or just about any other mild cheese. You can use any color pepper for this, as long as it's sweet and not fiery.

½ cup olive oil
2 pounds green bell pepper, or any sweet pepper, seeds and membranes removed and cut into quarters

½ cup dry sherry
2 tablespoons vinegar
Salt to taste
½ teaspoon lemon juice

Put the olive oil in a large skillet, lay the peppers in, skin side down, and cook slowly over medium-low heat until brown, about 10 minutes. Add the sherry, vinegar, and salt, cover, and cook 10 minutes more. Remove from the heat and let cool. Drain and reserve the peppers, putting only the olive oil mixture in a bowl, and add the lemon juice. Cut the peppers into ¼-inch strips and stir them into the olive oil mixture. Keep in the refrigerator until ready to use.

Chow Chow

(seven cups)

Chow chow was originally a Chinese sweetmeat made of orange peel, ginger, and other spices preserved in a thick syrup. Today chow chow is defined as any mixed vegetable pickle flavored with mustard or mustard seed. Chow chow has a flamboyant flavor that lights up roast chicken and lamb.

4 cups cauliflower flowerets
(⅓ to ½ head cauliflower)
2 cups coarsely chopped
cabbage (⅛ to ¼ head
cabbage)
1 cup cut-up cucumber
(sliced ¼ inch thick, and
cut into quarters)
1 sweet red pepper, coarsely
chopped

1 large onion, chopped
3 teaspoons salt
⅓ cup flour
1 tablespoon dry mustard
1 teaspoon ground turmeric
1½ cups sugar
3 cups white vinegar

Bring a large pot of salted water to a boil. Blanch the cauliflower, cabbage, cucumber, red pepper, and onion: Put the vegetables in a strainer, one kind at a time, and lower into the boiling water. Leave for about 5 seconds, remove, and drain. Put the vegetables into a large bowl.

Mix together the salt, flour, mustard, turmeric, sugar, and 1 cup of the vinegar in a small pan, and stir briskly until blended. Cook over low heat for a few minutes, stirring constantly, then add the remaining 2 cups of vinegar, and continue to cook until smooth and thick. Remove from the heat.

Fill clean jars with the vegetables and spoon the mustard mixture over them to cover. Put lids on the jars and refrigerate. Use within a month.

Real Relish

(four cups)

A relish that has withstood the test of time, from a recipe that's been around since at least the 1920s. It's a benchmark for basic relish. It's sweet and spicy, and the best relish for beef.

1 pound tomatoes, chopped   1 cup cider vinegar
1 medium onion, chopped   1 cup sugar
2 stalks celery, chopped   2 teaspoons mustard seed
1 green bell pepper, chopped   1 tablespoon pickling spice
Salt to taste, plus 1 teaspoon

Put the tomatoes, onion, celery, and green pepper in a large bowl, lightly salt, and toss and mix until blended.

Put the vinegar, sugar, mustard seed, pickling spice, and the teaspoon salt in a saucepan and bring to a boil. Reduce the heat and let the pickling brine simmer for 2 or 3 minutes. Remove from the heat and strain the hot brine over the vegetable mixture. Stir, then put the relish into clean jars. Cover and refrigerate until needed.

Corn Relish

(six cups)

This relish is as corny as Kansas in August. Open a jar when you're serving Roast Chicken with Smothered Potatoes (see page 71), or use it when you're eating a mild dish that needs sprucing up.

4 cups corn kernels, fresh (about 6 ears) or frozen	2 teaspoons dry mustard
1½ green bell peppers, chopped	2 teaspoons ground turmeric
5 to 6 stalks of celery, chopped	2 teaspoons celery seed
2 medium onions, chopped	2½ cups white vinegar
1 cup sugar	¼ cup water

If you're using fresh corn, cut the kernels from the cob with a sharp knife. Mix together the corn kernels, bell peppers, celery, onions, sugar, mustard, turmeric, celery seed, vinegar, and water in a large pot and bring to a boil. Reduce the heat to simmer, and cook 15 minutes.

Put the hot corn relish into clean jars, cover, and when cool refrigerate. Will keep for a month. For longer preserving, fill sterilized jars with the hot mixture, leaving ½-inch headspace. Put on the lids and tighten, and process in a boiling-water canner for 10 minutes.

Fire and Ice Relish

(about five cups)

This relish was all the rage during the 1940s. Little dishes of Fire and Ice Relish kept dainty lunches company in tearooms all over California.

3 cups cherry tomatoes	1½ teaspoons mustard seed
1 large green bell pepper	4 teaspoons sugar
1 large red onion	⅛ teaspoon cayenne pepper
¼ cup cider vinegar	½ teaspoon black pepper
½ teaspoon salt	¼ cup water
1½ teaspoons celery seed	

Cut the cherry tomatoes in half, or, if they are large, into quarters, and put in a bowl. Seed and coarsely chop the bell pepper and add to the tomatoes. Finely chop the onion and add to the tomatoes.

Mix together the cider vinegar, salt, celery seed, mustard seed, sugar, cayenne pepper, black pepper, and water in a small saucepan and bring to a boil. Boil for 1 minute. Remove from the heat and immediately pour over the prepared vegetables. Cool, then cover and refrigerate at least 3 hours before serving. This is a fresh relish and will keep no more than a day or two.

Rhubarb-Onion Relish

(six cups)

Serve this relish cold, rather than at room temperature. It makes an agreeable contrast to a hot meat dish like Black Pepper Ribs (see page 102).

2 cups chopped rhubarb	2 cups light brown sugar
4 medium white onions, chopped	½ teaspoon ground cloves
(2 cups)	½ teaspoon allspice
1 cup vinegar	½ teaspoon cinnamon
1½ teaspoons salt	

Mix together the rhubarb, onions, vinegar, salt, brown sugar, cloves, allspice, and cinnamon in a large heavy-bottomed pot, bring to a boil, and simmer for 45 minutes, until the relish is quite thick.

Put the relish into clean jars, cover, and when cool refrigerate. For longer preserving, fill sterilized jars with the hot mixture, leaving ¼-inch headspace. Put on the lids and tighten, and process in a boiling-water canner for 15 minutes.

Piccalilli

(seven cups)

I have no idea how this East Indian relish got to New England, where it was traditionally served with Boston Baked Beans (see page 111), but the tradition is worth upholding.

1½ pounds firm unripe tomatoes, coarsely chopped (4 cups)
4 to 5 stalks celery, chopped
1 green bell pepper, chopped
1 sweet red pepper, chopped
2 cups chopped cauliflower
(⅛ head cauliflower)
2 large yellow onions, chopped

5 cups cider vinegar
3 cups sugar
3 teaspoons celery seed
1½ tablespoons mustard seed
¾ teaspoon cinnamon
¾ teaspoon allspice
2 teaspoons salt, or to taste

Put the tomatoes, celery, peppers, cauliflower, and onions in a large kettle, add 2 cups of the vinegar, bring to a boil, and simmer for 1 minute. Drain well. In another pot, put the remaining 3 cups vinegar and the sugar, celery seed, mustard seed, cinnamon, allspice, and salt, bring to a boil, and simmer for 10 minutes.

Spoon the vegetables into jars, and pour the marinade over; cover and when cool refrigerate. For longer preserving, fill sterilized jars with the hot mixture, leaving ¼-inch headspace. Put on the lids and tighten, and process in a boiling-water canner for 15 minutes.

Wirtabel's Melon Chutney

(eight cups)

This is the chutney my friend Wirtabel's family made every year with the melons on their farm that didn't ripen properly. It is excellent, and it beats mango chutney by a mile, as well as being far less expensive to make.

12 cups fruit, peeled, seeded, and diced. Use about 6 cups melon, cantaloupe or honeydew (either ripe or unripe), cut into 1-inch cubes; the remaining fruit may be pear, apple, or peach
2 cups raisins (1 cup golden raisins and 1 cup dark raisins, mixed)

1 cup peeled chopped fresh ginger
4½ cups sugar
3 cups white vinegar
1 teaspoon whole allspice
½ teaspoon whole cloves
2 cinnamon sticks, each 2 inches long

Mix together the fruit, raisins, ginger, sugar, and vinegar in a large Dutch oven or kettle. Tie the allspice, cloves, and cinnamon sticks in a piece of cheesecloth. Use a hammer to smash the spices in the cheesecloth a couple of times to release more flavor during cooking. Add to the kettle.

Bring the mixture to a boil, stirring occasionally. Reduce heat to simmer, and cook for about 2 hours, or until thickened and darker. Taste occasionally to check on the need for more spices or sugar or salt. When thick and darker, remove from the heat and discard the spice bag.

Put the hot chutney into clean jars, cover, and when cool refrig-

erate; will keep for up to a month. For longer preserving, fill sterilized jars with the hot mixture, leaving ¼-inch headspace. Put on
the lids and tighten, and process in a boiling-water canner for 15
minutes.

Applesauce

(four servings)

The best applesauce you ever tasted can be made from the new
crop of Gravenstein apples that appear in the market in late August
or early September; but don't hesitate to try other varieties as well.
(I don't recommend Delicious apples because they are very sweet.)
Warm applesauce makes a grand dessert with vanilla ice cream,
heavy cream, or a dusting of cinnamon.

8 apples, peeled, cored, and cut into eighths (use Graven- steins, if possible)	Sugar to taste
	2 tablespoons lemon juice
	1 tablespoon finely chopped
½ cup water	lemon zest

Put the apples and water into a heavy-bottomed pan; cook over low
heat, stirring occasionally, until the apples begin to get tender. Add
a little sugar—be sparing until the apples mash easily. (Most
Gravensteins are so sweet they need very little sugar.) Add the
lemon juice and cook until the applesauce is soft enough to be
mashed with a fork.

Remove from the heat, add the lemon zest, and mash with the
tines of a fork, leaving some coarse texture. Serve warm or cold.

Fried Apple Rings

(two servings)

Rings of apple sautéed gently in a little butter are the garnish you need for just about any ham or pork dish. You can make a lot of Apple Rings and keep them in the refrigerator for a day or two. Spread them out on a baking sheet and reheat them in the oven just before serving.

4 tablespoons (½ stick) butter   3 tablespoons sugar
1 medium-large firm apple,   1 teaspoon cinnamon
   cored and sliced into six or
   seven ¼- to ½-inch rings

Melt the butter in a large skillet over medium heat, then place the apple rings in a single layer in the skillet. Mix together the sugar and cinnamon, and sprinkle over the apple rings. Cook for 2 minutes, then turn the apple rings over and reduce the heat to very low. Cover the skillet and cook for 2 or 3 more minutes. Test for doneness. Some of the rings will be tender—stack those on top of the ones that need another minute. Add more rings as needed to the skillet without using more butter, but continue to sprinkle on the sugar/cinnamon coating. Serve warm.

Baby Peas and Iceberg Lettuce

(four to six servings)

Iceberg lettuce lifts the garden pea to new heights. Because of the lettuce, you're able to cook the peas in less water, and they don't lose their delicate flavor.

4 pounds unshelled petite
green peas (about 4 cups
shelled)
6 tablespoons (¾ stick) butter
1 small head iceberg lettuce,
cored, rinsed, wrapped, and
chilled (see page 11), cut
into julienne strips

Salt and pepper to taste
1 teaspoon sugar
½ cup water

Shell the peas. Heat the butter in a saucepan, add the peas and lettuce, salt and pepper, sugar, and water; stir to mix well. Bring to a boil and quickly reduce heat to a simmer. Cover and simmer for about 5 minutes, or until the peas are tender—the timing depends on the age of the peas. Serve hot.

Blanche's Cabbage with Bacon

(four servings)

Cabbage blanched for just twelve seconds turns a lovely celery-green color. This is *the* dish to have with sausage and rye bread. A small head of cabbage torn into bite-size pieces looks like a huge amount, but it wilts and cooks down to serve four ordinary appetites.

1 medium head cabbage, 2 to 2½ pounds (about 16 cups prepared)	4 tablespoons bacon fat (from cooking bacon)
¼ pound bacon, diced	4 tablespoons cider vinegar
½ teaspoon sugar	Salt to taste

Core the cabbage and carefully separate the leaves. Remove the thick center vein from each leaf and tear the leaves into large bite-size pieces.

Bring a large pot of water to a boil. In a small skillet, slowly cook the diced bacon until it is golden brown. Remove the bacon and drain on a paper towel. Save 4 tablespoons of bacon fat, mix it together with the sugar, and set aside. Plunge the cabbage into the boiling water and blanch for 12 seconds. Immediately drain the cabbage and toss in a bowl with the bacon, the sugar mixture, and the vinegar. Add salt and serve.

Carrots with Fresh Mint

(four servings)

Carrots with Fresh Mint is like having supper in the garden. There is a real difference between eating a whole mint leaf and little snippets of one. Leave them whole and bring the garden right to your plate.

1 pound carrots (about 5 medium), peeled and sliced ¼ inch thick 2 cups water Salt to taste	3 tablespoons butter 2 teaspoons brown sugar ⅓ cup whole fresh mint leaves, small if possible

Put the carrots, water, and salt in a saucepan and bring to a boil. Turn the heat to low and cook for about 5 minutes, or until the carrots are just tender. Remove from the heat and drain.

Melt the butter and sugar over low heat in a skillet. Add the carrots, stirring and tossing for about 1 minute to coat with the butter mixture. Put the carrots in a serving dish and toss with the fresh mint leaves. Serve.

Cornmeal-Fried Tomatillos

(about thirty slices)

A tomatillo looks exactly like a shiny miniature green tomato hidden by an ugly husk. You find these tangy-tasting fruits in the
supermarket the year round. As a fringe dish, tomatillos have the
same complementary effect lemon does on black beans or fish and
chicken dishes.

15 medium or large tomatillos	2 tablespoons vegetable oil
¾ cup yellow cornmeal	Salt and pepper to taste

Remove the husks from the tomatillos, cut off the tops and bot-
toms, and slice ½ inch thick. Spread the cornmeal on a large piece
of waxed paper and coat both sides of the tomatillo slices with the
cornmeal.

Put the oil in a 12-inch skillet and heat until quite hot. *Quickly*
place the tomatillo slices in a single layer in the skillet. As soon as
all of the slices are in the pan, lightly salt and pepper, and begin
turning them over. Cook just a few seconds, and remove from the
heat. The tomatillos must not cook longer than a few seconds or
they will become mushy. Serve right away.

Jasmine Rice

(six servings)

I love the delicate fragrance of jasmine, but I never tasted it in food until I finally figured out how to put it there. I tried different methods until I succeeded with this. You'll find that this rice is perfectly tuned to white fish and seafood. The jasmine tea leaves must be fragrant when you smell them or they won't impart anything to the rice, so check yours before you make this.

2 teaspoons jasmine tea leaves	1½ teaspoons salt
3½ cups water	1½ cups long-grain white rice

If you are using teabags, cut them open and measure out 2 teaspoons of tea. Put the tea leaves in a small processor and process until they are tiny flecks, or use a mortar and pestle.

Put the water and salt in a saucepan and bring to a boil. Add the tea, and slowly add the rice. Shake the pan to level the rice and turn the heat down to simmer. Cover the pan and allow to cook for 15 minutes, or until the rice is tender. Remove from the heat, mix with a fork to fluff, and serve hot.

Orzo with Fresh Dill

(four servings)

Orzo is one of the kinds of pasta that look like rice. It was James Beard's favorite pasta to serve with lamb, and it's a favorite of mine with fish. You can have just plain orzo for supper, too, mixed with grated cheese, or salsa.

1 cup orzo pasta	2 tablespoons butter
⅓ cup chopped fresh dill	Salt to taste

Bring 4 quarts of salted water to a boil in a large pot. Add the orzo and cook for about 8 minutes, or until tender, stirring occasionally. Drain the orzo and put in a bowl. Add 2 tablespoons of the dill and the butter, and stir until the butter is melted. Salt to taste and serve hot. Pass around the rest of the dill to sprinkle over each serving.

Deviled Eggs

(four eggs)

I'm always happy when I see deviled eggs served. They please most people and add substance and heartiness to a supper of salad or soup that might not otherwise be filling enough.

4 eggs	1 teaspoon ball-park mustard
4 tablespoons mayonnaise	Black pepper to taste

Pierce the large end of each egg with an egg piercer or a needle; this will release the pressure that often cracks the shell. Put the eggs in a pan and fill it with water. Bring to a boil, and simmer for 15 minutes.

Remove from the heat and place the eggs in cold water immediately. (An overcooked egg yolk develops a harmless dark ring that isn't as appetizing as the bright yellow yolk.) Shell the eggs, cut in half lengthwise, and gently remove the yolks.

Put the yolks in a small bowl, mash with a fork, and stir in the mayonnaise, mustard, and pepper. Fill the hard-boiled egg whites with the mixture and serve.

Coleslaw

(six servings)

All-American coleslaw in a plain and simple version that's the best one I've found.

⅓ head green savoy cabbage, finely shredded (5 cups)
2 to 3 stalks celery, finely chopped

Salt and pepper to taste

Coleslaw Dressing
½ cup mayonnaise
¼ teaspoon salt

½ teaspoon sugar
1 tablespoon cider vinegar

Put the cabbage and celery in a bowl and salt and pepper to taste.

Blend together the mayonnaise, salt, sugar, and vinegar until smooth. Pour over the cabbage and celery, mix well, and refrigerate until needed.

L.A. Slaw

(six servings)

There are lots of Salvadoran restaurants in Los Angeles that serve
papusas (see page 134), slightly plump little tortillas filled with spicy
meat or cheese. This is the peppy slaw that goes along with them.

¾ cup white vinegar
6 tablespoons vegetable oil
4 cloves garlic, finely chopped
   and mixed with ⅓ cup ice
   water
½ teaspoon Tabasco sauce, or
   to taste

1½ tablespoons chili powder
1½ teaspoons salt, or to taste
1 head green savoy cabbage,
   chopped into small pieces

Put the vinegar, oil, garlic in ice water, Tabasco, chili powder, and
salt in a large mixing bowl. Mix very well. Add the cabbage and
toss and stir until it is well coated with the dressing. Cover and chill
and use as needed. This keeps well.

Turnip Slaw

(six servings)

The turnip is a neglected root, a vegetable that is never discussed, and rarely seen in public. Here it gets its proper due in a recipe that sets off the little bite in its flavor and the little crunch of its texture. Use it wherever you would use coleslaw.

½ cup mayonnaise
3 tablespoons sour cream
2 teaspoons tarragon vinegar
1 teaspoon prepared mustard
1 teaspoon sugar
Dash of salt

¼ teaspoon celery seed
¼ teaspoon pepper
1 teaspoon chopped fresh dill;
  or ½ teaspoon dried dill
1 pound white turnip, peeled
  and shredded (4 cups)

In a large bowl, stir together the mayonnaise, sour cream, tarragon vinegar, mustard, sugar, salt, celery seed, pepper, dill, and turnip. Mix well and refrigerate until needed.

Tiny Herb Salads

(six to eight servings)

Here is an exciting and novel idea that's become fashionable in some Parisian restaurants: tiny portions of intensely flavored salads made from one or more fresh herbs and served alongside main courses as a fresh condiment. This is an extremely simple way for you to get to know herbs: which herbs go together, which herbs go with what. Your palate should be your guide: getting a working knowledge of herbs and their qualities in this way is better than a shelf full of cookbooks.

Vinaigrette

4 tablespoons olive oil	½ teaspoon salt
2 teaspoons wine vinegar	1 teaspoon Dijon mustard
2 tablespoons cold water	

Salad

1 cup herb leaves and/or flowers, stems removed, leaves left whole (one or more of the following: thyme, sage, parsley, tarragon, marjoram, oregano, savory, chervil, basil, cilantro, dill . . .)

2 cups chopped iceberg lettuce
2 tablespoons finely chopped green onions or scallions

Put all of the vinaigrette ingredients in a jar and shake vigorously until thoroughly blended. Set the dressing aside while preparing the salad.

Select the herb or herbs you want to enhance your supper. Toss the lettuce, onions, and herbs in a bowl. Pour the vinaigrette over the salad, toss, and serve about ½ cup salad per person.

Crouton Salad

(four servings)

This is for people who feel there are never enough croutons in their salad. Instead of a green salad with only three croutons per serving, here, finally, is a crouton salad with just a few greens. The important thing to know is that a Crouton Salad could take the place of rice or potatoes or a dinner roll with your supper. And of course you can change the greens to suit the main supper dish; in place of parsley and celery, try baby spinach leaves, for example.

½ cup olive oil
2 cloves garlic, put through a
   garlic press
Salt to taste
4 cups dried bread cubes,
   1 to 2 inches square

2 cups loosely packed Italian
   flat-leaf parsley sprigs
½ cup finely chopped scallions
2 tablespoons red wine vinegar
Optional: 1 cup celery leaves

Heat the oil and garlic in a large skillet over medium heat for 1 minute. Liberally salt the bread cubes, then add them to the skillet and heat for another minute or two, stirring and turning them over until they are lightly browned. Remove from the heat, add the parsley, scallions, vinegar, and optional celery leaves. Toss and serve immediately.

Cucumber Salad

(four servings)

Whenever something sweet and sour and fresh is called for, Cucumber Salad is usually it. The light and puckery dressing for this little salad is the simplest form of a pickle solution. Serve on a leaf of butter lettuce as the side salad with a fish dish or with something as basic as crackers and cheese.

¾ cup water
1½ teaspoons salt
⅓ cup sugar
1½ tablespoons white vinegar

2 medium cucumbers, peeled, seeded, and sliced
A few leaves of butter lettuce

Mix together the water, salt, sugar, and vinegar in a bowl. Add the cucumbers and stir. Put in the refrigerator until ready to serve. Remove the cucumbers from the dressing and serve on the leaves of butter lettuce.

Lettuce in Cream

(four servings)

This dish is just right the way it is. You shouldn't touch it with salt and pepper. And don't be dismayed by the cream—just remember that there is a lot of lettuce. Lettuce in Cream goes well with a plainly cooked rich fish, like salmon.

1 medium head iceberg lettuce,
  cored, rinsed, wrapped, and
  chilled (see page 11)

¼ cup sugar
¼ cup white vinegar
¾ cup light cream

Cut the lettuce into large pieces. Put the sugar, vinegar, and cream in a large mixing bowl and stir to blend well.

Ten minutes before serving, put the lettuce in the bowl and toss to coat the leaves. Serve on individual salad plates.

Wedge of Iceberg with Thick Creamy Dressing

(four servings)

Iceberg lettuce would smile if it could. It is a perfect creation, round and crisp and sturdy, despite its delicate flavor, and unlike some of the frail field lettuces that wilt, swoon, and have the vapors readily. My dog, Rover, loves it, especially dunked in meat drippings. He wouldn't touch arugula with a ten-foot pole. When made properly, this salad is as great as Caesar salad.

½ cup sour cream
½ cup mayonnaise
2 scallions, finely chopped
2 to 3 tablespoons lemon
   juice
½ cup crumbled Roquefort or
   other blue cheese

Pepper to taste
1 head iceberg lettuce, cored,
   rinsed, wrapped, and chilled
   (see page 11)

Put the sour cream, mayonnaise, scallions, and lemon juice in a bowl and stir until well blended. If too thick, add a little vegetable oil. Stir in the crumbled cheese, and pepper to taste. Refrigerate at least 4 hours before serving.

Cut the lettuce into 4 thick wedges and spoon about 6 tablespoons of dressing over each wedge.

Mustard Celery Salad

(four servings)

This dish that falls somewhere between a salad and a relish is a good way to round out a simple main course, such as fish.

6 to 7 stalks celery, cut into small dice (3 cups)	1 tablespoon prepared mustard (French's or ball-park)
1 cup finely chopped (loosely packed) parsley	Pepper to taste
½ cup mayonnaise	Butter lettuce leaves

Put the celery and parsley in a large bowl and toss. Stir the mayonnaise and mustard together until smooth, taste, and add more of either to balance the taste. Stir and toss into the celery mixture and add pepper to taste. Chill until needed. Serve on butter lettuce.

PUCCINI SPURNS THE SAVOY

" . . . [Chef] Francois Latry asked him to be allowed to prepare a rich Tuscan-style dish and name it after him. Puccini declined the honour on the grounds that it would give people a false impression of his eating habits, and his letters, indeed, testify to the simplicity of his tastes in this respect. For example, on 30 April 1880 he revealed to his younger brother: 'I worked till three o'clock this morning . . . Then I had a bunch of onions for supper.' Sometimes he would chop an onion very finely and enjoy it mixed with a can of tuna fish and its oil."

—from *Good Cheer*
by Frederick W. Hackwood

Relish Salad

(four servings)

Crunchy Relish Salad is a sweet-and-sour side dish that sharpens up the flavor of whatever gets served with it. It can be made in advance, even the day before.

½ teaspoon salt	⅛ head savoy cabbage,
3 tablespoons brown sugar	chopped (2 cups)
½ teaspoon dry mustard	½ green bell pepper, chopped
⅓ cup cider vinegar	2 to 3 stalks celery, chopped

Put the salt, brown sugar, dry mustard, and cider vinegar in a bowl and stir until blended. Add the cabbage, bell pepper, and celery and stir until all is well mixed. Serve chilled.

Grapefruit, Black Olive, and Mint Salad

(four servings)

I couldn't imagine how grapefruit, olives, and mint could commingle until I tried it. It turned out to be a striking sight, with a taste to match.

1 large grapefruit, peeled and	2 tablespoons olive oil
sectioned	1 teaspoon lemon juice
1 cup pitted black olives	¼ teaspoon salt, or to taste
1 cup whole fresh mint leaves	

To extract whole grapefruit sections, first put the fruit on a cutting board. Hold it firmly with one hand and with the other pare off the skin with a sharp knife. Cut away the white layer of pith beneath the skin as you pare. Remove the sections, cutting them away from the membrane, first on one side of a section, then the other. Cut off any white bits that remain and remove seeds, so that you have perfect whole segments of fruit.

Put the grapefruit segments, olives, and mint leaves in a bowl. Add the olive oil, lemon juice, and salt, and mix well.

Persimmon-Pear Salad

(six servings)

Pears and persimmons are kindred winter fruits that belong together in a salad like this one. The sliced fruit looks like flower petals tossed among the lettuces.

⅓ cup olive oil
2 tablespoons rice vinegar
1½ teaspoons Dijon mustard
½ teaspoon salt
2 tablespoons water
1 tablespoon sugar
2 Fuyu persimmons, peeled
   and sliced

2 pears (Bosc, if possible),
   peeled, cored, and sliced
4 cups mixed bitter green
   lettuces (such as curly
   endive, escarole, and
   chicory), washed and
   dried

Put the olive oil, vinegar, mustard, salt, water, and sugar in a large bowl and blend until well mixed. Then add the persimmons, pears, and lettuce and toss until well coated.

Welsh Rabbit

" . . . at the beach the same dish was very pleasant for supper when the air was brisk or the fog swept in from the sea. It was often made in a chafing dish and sometimes over a low wood fire in a heavy casserole or saucepan. With it went quantities of hot, hot toast, well buttered and crisp, and enormous amounts of beer. Knowing that some delicate appetites were not equal to so heavy a dish for late supper, Mother and Let always provided an alternate dish of chicken with a light cream sauce and mushrooms, flavored with a good deal of sherry . . . As a conclusion to this supper a light fruit dessert . . . "

—from *Delights and Prejudices*
by James Beard

Desserts

Beginner's Coconut Pie
Joyce's Paper Lemon Cookies
Black and White Chocolate
  Cookies
Crisp Ginger Cookies
Lemon Teasers
Oatmeal Raisin Cookies
Fresh Orange Cookies
Plain Jane Sugar Cookies
Almond Diamonds
Parker Brownies
Joyce's Almond Cakes
Sharon's Orange Scone Berry
  Cakes
Orange Sour Cream Cake
Chocolate Brownie Cake
Pineapple Upside-Down
  Cake
The Best Rice Pudding
Creamy *Riso* Pudding
Spanish Cream
Apple-Walnut Pudding

Bread Pudding
Chocolate Pudding
Baked Vanilla Custard
Brown Sugar Custard
Apples in Custard
Wine Jelly
Pralines
Pineapple Blizzard
Grapefruit Ice
Chilled Marmalade Grapefruit
Sautéed Pears
Maple Persimmons
Grapes with Sour Cream and
  Brown Sugar
Berry Sandwiches
Peach on Sugared Toast
Baked Plums and Apricots with
  Almonds
Baked Bananas with Berries or
  Mango
Rhubarb and Kumquat
  Compote

For me a meal is never quite finished without dessert. I have always loved sweets. Baking cookies and cakes is still an adventure for me. A little flour, salt, sugar, eggs, and butter; some brisk stirring; into the oven—and there is an amazing transformation into golden cookies and lofty cakes. One puts in so little for such great returns.

When I was growing up in La Crescenta, California, we always had the same dessert every night during the summer. Long summer evenings, after breathlessly hot days, meant sitting in the porch swing and eating ice cream. It seemed like everyone in our small foothill town retired to their front porch after supper to watch the stars come out and catch any little breeze that rippled by. Around eight o'clock, couples and families would begin to stroll down to Mr. Watson's drugstore to buy a quart of ice cream. He had chocolate, vanilla, strawberry, tutti frutti, and spumoni. I never knew anyone who bought tutti frutti or spumoni. My memory of Mr. Watson's ice cream is that it was perfect, and we never became tired of the same dessert every night. It was as good in August as it was in June.

There are no recipes for ice cream in this book because you can buy very good ice cream everywhere, but it is seldom that you can buy anything nearly as good as the Almond Diamond cookies (see page 210), the Parker Brownies (see page 211), the Fresh Orange Cookies (see page 208), or the Pineapple Upside-Down Cake (see page 216) in the pages that follow.

Beginner's Coconut Pie

(one 9- or 10-inch pie)

This is a mouth-watering, creamy custard baked in a pie plate *sans* crust, with golden crisp coconut on top. Slice in wedges, as you would any pie, and serve with a spoonful of unsweetened whipped cream.

2 cups milk	1¼ cups sugar
½ cup all-purpose flour	1½ teaspoons vanilla
1 teaspoon baking powder	1 cup grated sweetened
¼ teaspoon salt	coconut
4 eggs	

Preheat the oven to 350°F. Butter a 9- or 10-inch pie pan.

Put the milk, flour, baking powder, salt, eggs, sugar, and vanilla into a blender or food processor. Blend for 3 minutes. Add the coconut and blend for 2 or 3 seconds more. Pour the mixture into the pie pan. Bake for 30 to 35 minutes, or until the edges are set and the center trembles a trifle. Remove from the oven and let cool, or serve warm. If cooling and serving later, refrigerate, and warm a bit before serving.

Joyce's Paper Lemon Cookies

(about fifty cookies)

My friend Joyce McGillis is a fine home cook and she created these cookies—they're crisp and paper-thin, with an intense lemon flavor.

¾ cup (1½ sticks) unsalted butter, softened
1¼ cups sugar
1 teaspoon vanilla
2 tablespoons grated lemon rind
¼ cup freshly squeezed lemon juice

1½ cups all-purpose flour
1½ teaspoons baking powder
½ teaspoon baking soda
½ teaspoon salt
Optional: raw sugar for sprinkling on top

In a bowl, cream the butter and sugar together (an electric mixer is almost a must for the recipe). Add the vanilla, lemon rind, and lemon juice and continue to beat until smooth. Mix or sift together into another bowl the flour, baking powder, baking soda, and salt. Add to the butter and sugar mixture and blend well. Turn the dough out onto waxed paper or plastic wrap and form it into 2 logs about 1 to 1½ inches in diameter and about a foot long. Refrigerate for at least 2 hours, or wrap tightly and freeze until ready to use.

Preheat the oven to 350°F. Don't grease the cookie sheets.

Cut the logs into about ⅛-inch slices (less than ¼ inch) with a sharp knife, and place cookies about 3 inches apart on the cookie sheets. Sprinkle with raw sugar, if desired. Cut only enough cookies to fill the cookie sheets, then return the uncut dough to the refrigerator to keep chilled. (I put only 6 to 8 cookies on a sheet at a time to keep them from spreading together when baking.) Bake for

7 to 8 minutes, or until the cookies are lightly golden. Watch carefully during the last 1 to 2 minutes of cooking. Remove from the oven and let cool slightly on the cookie sheets before removing to racks to finish cooling.

Black and White Chocolate Cookies

(about two and one-half to three dozen cookies)

These little chocolate domes, crackled on top, are crisp outside and slightly chewy inside. These are nice, rich cookies after a supper salad.

3 ounces (3 squares) unsweetened chocolate
1 cup granulated sugar
6 tablespoons (¾ stick) butter,
room temperature
2 teaspoons vanilla

2 eggs
1 cup all-purpose flour
1¼ teaspoons baking powder
¼ teaspoon salt
⅓ cup confectioners' sugar,
sifted

Put the chocolate in a pan over barely simmering water until it has melted. Remove from the heat.

Put the sugar, butter, chocolate, and vanilla in a mixing bowl and stir to blend. Add the eggs and mix briskly until well blended. Add the flour, baking powder, and salt and stir until well mixed. Cover and refrigerate at least 3 hours or overnight.

Preheat the oven to 350°F. Don't grease the cookie sheets.

Sift the confectioners' sugar onto a large piece of waxed paper. Shape the cookie dough into rounded teaspoon-size balls and roll them in the confectioners' sugar. Place about 2 inches apart on cookie sheets. Bake for about 10 to 12 minutes, or until the top of the cookies feels almost firm to the touch. Remove from the oven and let cool for about 10 minutes before removing from the cookie sheets. Cool on racks.

Crisp Ginger Cookies

(about three and one-half dozen 2-inch cookies)

Paper-thin Crisp Ginger Cookies go especially well with papaya, mango, pineapple, or banana.

½ cup (1 stick) butter, softened
1 cup sugar
1 tablespoon ground ginger
½ teaspoon salt

½ cup milk
2 cups all-purpose flour
Optional: 1 cup coarsely
    chopped candied ginger

Preheat the oven to 350°F. Grease two cookie sheets.

Cream the butter and sugar together in a mixing bowl. Add the ground ginger, salt, and milk to the butter mixture and mix well. Slowly add the flour and blend well.

On the 2 greased cookie sheets spread the dough very thin, using a spatula or your hands. It helps to wet your fingers in cold water so the dough doesn't stick to your hands. If desired, scatter the chopped candied ginger over the dough; gently roll or pat the ginger into the dough. Bake for 20 to 25 minutes, or until lightly browned. While still hot, cut the cookies into 2-inch squares and remove from the pans. The cookies will be very thin and crisp.

Lemon Teasers

(sixteen 2-inch squares)

Butter crust covered with sharp lemon custard and dusted with confectioners' sugar, this cookie is a version of an old recipe from the era when every Junior League cookbook had lemon bars with names like "Melting Moments" and "Love Notes."

1 cup flour
⅓ cup confectioners' sugar; plus a little more to dust the top of the cookies
½ cup (1 stick) butter, chilled and cut into bits
2 eggs

¾ cup granulated sugar
½ teaspoon salt
¼ cup freshly squeezed lemon juice
2 tablespoons flour
½ teaspoon baking powder

Preheat the oven to 350°F. Butter an 8 × 8 × 2-inch baking pan.

Put the 1 cup flour and ⅓ cup confectioners' sugar in a bowl and, using a fork, stir to mix well. Add the bits of butter and, using your fingers, rub the butter and flour together until the mixture resembles coarse bread crumbs. Pat the mixture into the bottom of the baking pan. Bake for about 10 to 15 minutes, or until it is light golden. Remove from the oven.

Put the eggs into a mixing bowl and beat until they are thick and pale. Add the sugar, salt, and lemon juice and beat until well blended. Add the 2 tablespoons flour and the baking powder and beat until thoroughly mixed.

Pour the mixture over the partially baked crust and bake for about 15 minutes, or until the custard is light golden. Remove from the oven and dust the top with confectioners' sugar. Cool and cut into 16 squares.

Oatmeal Raisin Cookies

(about four dozen 2-inch round cookies)

These are homey, coarse cookies with oatmeal and raisins. They are satisfying between meals, and they go with puddings at suppertime, too.

1 cup sugar	1 teaspoon baking soda
½ cup (1 stick) butter, softened	1 teaspoon salt
⅓ cup honey	2 cups rolled oats
2 eggs	1 cup raisins
1¾ cups all-purpose flour	

Preheat the oven to 350°F. Grease the cookie sheets.

Mix the sugar, butter, and honey in a large bowl, beating until the mixture is creamy and smooth. Add the eggs and beat well. Stir in the flour, baking soda, and salt. Mix well. Add the oats and raisins and stir until well mixed.

Drop tablespoonfuls of the dough 2 inches apart on the cookie sheets. Flatten each mound of dough with your fingertips. If the dough sticks, occasionally dip your fingers in a bowl of cold water to prevent sticking. Bake for about 8 to 10 minutes, or until the cookies are light brown. Remove from the oven and cool about 5 minutes on the cookie sheets. Remove the cookies to finish cooling on a rack, and store in an airtight container. These cookies freeze well: Put in plastic bags, close with a twist tie, and freeze until needed.

Fresh Orange Cookies

(about three dozen 2-inch round cookies)

Here is a sugar cookie that doesn't have to be refrigerated, rolled out, cut out, re-refrigerated, and rerolled. It is awfully good when something sweet is needed.

1 cup (2 sticks) butter, softened
1 cup sugar
1 medium unpeeled orange, cut into pieces, seeds removed
½ lemon, cut into pieces, seeds removed

2 cups all-purpose flour
½ teaspoon baking soda
½ teaspoon salt

Icing
3 tablespoons butter, softened
2 cups confectioners' sugar, sifted

2 tablespoons finely chopped or ground orange and lemon (from above)
2 tablespoons orange juice

Preheat the oven to 350°F. Do not butter the cookie sheets.

Put the butter and sugar into a mixing bowl and beat until smooth and creamy. Finely chop the orange and lemon (or grind in the food processor). Put the ground or chopped orange and lemon into a strainer and press to extract excess juice. (Don't worry if you don't remove all the moisture.) There should be approximately 1 cup of ground or chopped orange and lemon. Add ½ cup, firmly packed, of the orange and lemon to the butter mixture and mix well. Reserve 2 tablespoons of the remaining orange and lemon for the icing and freeze the rest for some other use. Add the flour, baking soda, and salt and beat until well blended.

Drop the dough by tablespoons onto the cookie sheets, leaving 2 inches between. Flatten the dough with your fingers. If the dough is sticky, dip your fingers into cold water before pressing. Bake for 10 to 12 minutes, or until the cookies are golden. Remove to racks.

While the cookies are baking, make the icing. Cream together the butter and confectioners' sugar. Add the ground orange and lemon and the orange juice and beat until smooth. Spread on the top of the cookies while they are still warm.

Plain Jane Sugar Cookies

(about fifty 2½-inch round cookies)

A no-frills, all-purpose cookie, Plain Janes take just ten minutes to make and ten minutes to bake. You can eat them with fruit, or just by themselves, and they're good with chocolate ice cream.

½ cup butter (1 stick), room temperature	2 teaspoons vanilla
1 cup sugar	1½ cups all-purpose flour
1 egg, lightly beaten	1½ teaspoons baking powder
	½ teaspoon salt

Preheat the oven to 350°F. Grease the cookie sheets.

Cream the butter in a mixing bowl. Add the sugar and beat until blended and smooth. Stir in the egg and vanilla and mix well. Add the flour, baking powder, and salt, and stir until well mixed.

Drop well-rounded teaspoons of dough onto the cookie sheets about 2½ inches apart. Use the bottom of a glass or small cup to flatten the mounds of dough; begin by putting the bottom of the glass in dough to make it sticky and then dip the glass in sugar before pressing down each cookie. Repeat when stickiness disappears. Bake for 10 to 12 minutes, or until the edges of the cookies are light golden. Remove from the cookie sheets and cool on racks.

Almond Diamonds

(about thirty-two cookies)

Almond Diamonds are just a little fancier and more delicate than your everyday cookie. These diamonds aren't forever, though. They get eaten up fast, especially with fruit compotes, ice cream, or custards.

½ cup (1 stick) butter, room
  temperature
¾ cup sugar
1 egg, separated
1 teaspoon vanilla

1 cup sifted all-purpose flour
¼ teaspoon salt
½ cup coarsely chopped sliced
  almonds
½ teaspoon cinnamon

Preheat the oven to 400°F. Grease a 17 × 12 × 1-inch jelly-roll pan.

Cream together the butter and ½ cup of the sugar until very light. Beat in the egg yolk and vanilla, then gradually stir in the flour and salt. With a spatula dipped in cold water, spread the dough evenly and thinly over the bottom of the jelly-roll pan. (The dough is somewhat stiff, so dot spoonfuls of it all over the pan, then spread with the spatula.)

Beat the egg white until it is just stiff, then brush it all over the top of the dough. Mix together the almonds, cinnamon, and the remaining ¼ cup sugar. Sprinkle this mixture on top of the egg white. Bake for 8 to 10 minutes. The cookies are done when the edges are golden and shrinking away from the sides of the pan. Remove from the oven and immediately cut diagonally into diamond shapes, with each side of the diamonds measuring about 2½ inches. Cool and store in an airtight container.

Parker Brownies

(sixteen brownies)

I renamed these brownies after a young man who was crazy about them. He told me that when he was in Spain studying flamenco guitar, he imagined that if he had to, he could make a living making and selling these brownies.

2 ounces (2 squares) unsweetened chocolate
¼ cup (½ stick) butter
1 cup sugar
1 egg
⅛ teaspoon salt

½ cup all-purpose flour
½ cup chopped walnuts
1 teaspoon vanilla
Optional: confectioners'
  sugar for dusting

Preheat the oven to 300°F. Butter an 8-inch square baking pan. Line the bottom of the pan with waxed paper, then butter and flour the paper.

In a saucepan over very low heat, melt the chocolate with the butter, stirring to blend. Remove from the heat and stir in the sugar, egg, salt, flour, walnuts, and vanilla. Spread in the prepared pan and bake for about 30 minutes. Remove from the oven and cool for about 5 minutes, then turn out onto a rack and peel the waxed paper from the bottom. Transfer to a cutting board and cut into squares. Dust brownies with confectioners' sugar, if desired.

Joyce's Almond Cakes

(eight cakes)

These are small muffin-size dessert cakes that are tailored to go with fruits, especially berries.

½ cup (1 stick) butter, room
   temperature
¾ cup sugar
2 eggs, well beaten
1⅓ cups cake flour
2 teaspoons baking powder
¼ teaspoon salt
⅓ cup milk
1¼ cups coarsely chopped
   blanched almonds
Confectioners' sugar for
   dusting the tops of the cakes

Preheat the oven to 375°F. Butter 8 muffin tins well.

Cream the butter and sugar together until light and creamy. Add the eggs, beating thoroughly. Stir in the flour, baking powder, and salt; beat, then add the milk. Mix well and stir in the almonds.

Spoon the batter into the muffin tins, filling each two-thirds full. Bake for about 12 to 14 minutes, or until the center is dry when a straw is inserted. Dust the tops with confectioners' sugar. Serve warm.

"Who goes to bed supperless tosses all night."

—Italian proverb

Sharon's Orange Scone Berry Cakes

(fourteen cakes)

Sharon Kramis has never given me a recipe I didn't like. These little cakes are meant to be served as a supper dessert with a bowl of berries, but it's okay if you don't have the berries. They make an absolutely exemplary dessert by themselves, with just a cup of good coffee.

2 cups all-purpose flour less
   2 tablespoons
1 tablespoon baking powder
1 teaspoon salt
2 tablespoons plus ½ cup sugar
⅓ cup (⅔ stick) butter, chilled
1 egg, beaten

½ cup heavy cream
2 tablespoons butter, melted
2 tablespoons grated orange
   zest
Optional: fresh berries or
   berry preserves

Preheat the oven to 400°F.

In a bowl, stir together the flour, baking powder, salt, and the 2 tablespoons sugar. Using a pastry blender or two knives, cut the chilled butter into the flour mixture. Mix together the egg and cream in another bowl and add to the dry ingredients; stir until just blended.

Turn out onto a floured board and knead for 1 minute. Shape the dough into a rectangle that is 8 inches wide, 14 inches long, and ¼ inch thick. Brush on the melted butter, then sprinkle with the ½ cup sugar and orange zest. Roll up jelly-roll fashion from the longer, 14-inch side, and cut into 1-inch slices.

Arrange the slices, cut side down, on an ungreased baking sheet and bake for 10 to 12 minutes, or until lightly browned. Serve with butter and fresh berries or berry preserves.

Orange Sour Cream Cake

(one 8½ × 4½ × 3-inch loaf cake)

This recipe was a gift from Marlene Sorosky, a fine baker who used to have a Cake of the Month Club. (James Beard once told me that her cakes were the best he ever ate.) This one blooms with orange flavor, it's simple to make, and it keeps well.

½ cup (1 stick) butter, room temperature
¾ cup sugar
2 large eggs, separated (may also be added whole)
¼ teaspoon salt
1 teaspoon orange extract

1 teaspoon grated orange zest
1 cup all-purpose flour
½ teaspoon baking powder
½ teaspoon baking soda
½ cup plus 2 tablespoons sour cream
½ cup finely chopped walnuts

Preheat oven to 325°F. Grease and lightly flour a loaf pan.

Beat the butter and ½ cup of the sugar in a large mixing bowl until light, about 2 minutes. Add the yolks and beat well. (If using whole eggs, add them here and use all ¾ cup of the sugar.) Add orange extract and zest, and blend. Stir together the flour, baking powder, and baking soda in another bowl. Add alternately with the sour cream and beat until well mixed. Mix in the walnuts. Beat the egg whites and slowly add the remaining ¼ cup sugar to them; beat until the whites hold stiff peaks. Gently fold the whites into the batter, then spoon into the loaf pan.

Bake for about 40 to 50 minutes, or until a straw comes out clean when inserted in the center. Don't overbake! Cool on a rack.

Chocolate Brownie Cake

(four servings)

It's hard to believe that just six tablespoons of cocoa can make a chocolate cake so rich, dark, and moist. This cake will stay fresh longer than most. Serve it warm.

¼ cup (½ stick) butter, softened
½ cup plus ⅓ cup brown sugar
2 eggs
1 teaspoon vanilla
¾ cup all-purpose flour
¼ teaspoon salt
½ teaspoon baking soda

⅓ cup plus 1 tablespoon
   cocoa powder
2 tablespoons water
⅓ cup hot water
Confectioners' sugar for
   dusting the top of the cake
Heavy cream, softly whipped

Preheat the oven to 350°F. Grease an 8-inch square baking pan.

Cream together the butter and the ½ cup of brown sugar in a mixing bowl. Add the eggs and vanilla and mix until blended. In a small bowl, mix together the flour, salt, baking soda, and the ⅓ cup cocoa. Add the flour mixture to the butter mixture and blend. Stir in the 2 tablespoons water. Pour the batter into the baking pan. Mix together the remaining ⅓ cup brown sugar, 1 tablespoon cocoa, and the ⅓ cup hot water. Pour the hot water mixture over the batter.

Place the pan in a slightly larger ovenproof dish. Add 1 inch of boiling water to the larger dish and put into the oven. Bake for 20 to 25 minutes, or until a skewer comes out clean. Dust with confectioners' sugar. Serve with lightly whipped cream.

Pineapple Upside-Down Cake

(six to eight servings)

Pineapple Upside-Down Cake was my very favorite dessert as a child. I first remember my mother making it around 1928 for special occasions. She always lacked confidence in the kitchen, especially when baking, but this cake turned out perfect every time. It is a simple cake for a beginning baker.

¼ cup (½ stick) butter	1 teaspoon vanilla
¾ cup packed dark brown sugar	2 eggs
	1⅔ cups all-purpose flour
7 canned pineapple rings	2 teaspoons baking powder
7 maraschino cherries	¼ teaspoon salt
⅓ cup shortening	⅔ cup milk
⅔ cup granulated sugar	Whipped cream

Preheat the oven to 350°F.

Melt the butter over medium heat in a 9-inch cast-iron or other ovenproof skillet. Add the brown sugar and continue to cook, stirring constantly, until the sugar melts and is very thick and bubbly.

Arrange the pineapple rings in a single layer in the pan, pressing them down into the hot syrup. Place a cherry in the center of each ring. Set aside.

Cream the shortening in a large mixing bowl. Add the granulated sugar gradually, beating well. Add the vanilla and the eggs, and continue to beat until the mixture is well blended and light. Stir together the flour, baking powder, and salt in another bowl. Add to the creamed mixture along with the milk, beating about 30 seconds, until the batter is smooth. Spread evenly over the pineapple rings.

Bake for 35 to 40 minutes, or until a skewer comes out clean when inserted in the center of the cake, and thick, syrupy juices are bubbling around the edges. Remove from the oven and let cool for 5 minutes. Place a serving plate face down over skillet, turn both upside down, and remove the skillet. Serve warm with whipped cream.

The Best Rice Pudding

(six servings)

This is certainly the best rice pudding for today, because it short-cuts the old-fashioned method of cooking rice for hours and hours in large quantities of milk. Use short-grain rice because it's starchier than long-grain rice, and it makes a creamier pudding.

1 cup water	2 teaspoons vanilla
½ cup short-grain white rice	½ cup plus 2 tablespoons
½ teaspoon salt	sugar
2 cups milk	2 eggs
½ cup golden raisins	¼ teaspoon cinnamon
1 cup heavy cream	Optional: heavy cream

Preheat the oven to 350°F. Butter an 8-inch square baking dish.

Bring the water to a boil in a 2-quart saucepan. Add the rice and salt. Cover and cook over low heat for 10 minutes. Add the milk and the raisins, cover, and cook over low heat for 10 to 15 minutes more, or until the rice is tender.

In a small bowl, blend the cream, vanilla, sugar, and eggs. Add to the rice. Pour into the baking dish, and sprinkle with the cinnamon. Place in a slightly larger ovenproof dish. Add 1 inch of boiling water to the larger dish and place in the oven. Bake for 30 to 45 minutes. Serve at room temperature with heavy cream if desired.

Creamy Riso Pudding

(four to six servings)

This is the creamiest rice pudding you've ever eaten, because it's made with *riso* (or orzo), the pasta that impersonates rice. It's better than the real thing.

½ cup *riso* (or orzo) pasta (this makes 2 cups cooked)	2 egg yolks
	1½ teaspoons vanilla
2 cups milk	½ cup golden raisins
½ cup sugar	Nutmeg to sprinkle lightly on
½ teaspoon salt	top of baked pudding
1 egg	Heavy cream

Preheat the oven to 350°F. Butter an 8-inch square baking dish.

Bring a pot of salted water to a boil. Stir in the *riso* and cook, stirring occasionally, for 10 minutes, or until the pasta is tender. Drain and set aside.

Put the milk and 6 tablespoons of the sugar into a pan and bring to a simmer. Add the salt, stir, and remove from the heat. Lightly blend together the whole egg and egg yolks, and pour a little of the blended eggs over the hot milk, stirring constantly. Add the remaining eggs and stir briskly. Return the pan to the heat and cook a minute or two, stirring constantly. Remove from the heat and whisk the cooked *riso* into the milk mixture. Add the vanilla and raisins, and whisk until any little clumps of *riso* are separated. Pour into the buttered baking dish and bake for about 30 to 35 minutes, or until just set. Remove from the oven and sprinkle the top with nutmeg and the remaining 2 tablespoons of sugar. Serve warm with cream.

Spanish Cream

(four servings)

Spanish cream was among the recipes in the first *Fannie Farmer Cookbook*, written in 1896. Many early American cookbooks include Spanish cream, Spanish rice, and Spanish omelet as daring and exotic additions to their collections of mild Anglo-Saxon recipes. Spanish Cream (the Spanish touch is the addition of sherry wine) is a lovely, light chilled dessert.

1 envelope unflavored gelatin	2 eggs, separated, yolks lightly
¼ cup cold water	beaten with a fork
2 cups milk	4 tablespoons dry sherry
½ cup sugar	½ cup heavy cream
¼ teaspoon salt	

Sprinkle the gelatin over the cold water, stir, and let soften for 5 minutes.

Put the milk and sugar in a heavy-bottomed saucepan and heat until a tiny ring of bubbles forms around the edge of the pan. Remove from the heat, stir in the salt, and slowly pour the hot milk mixture over the egg yolks, stirring constantly. Pour back into the saucepan, add the softened gelatin, and cook over low heat, stirring until the custard thickens. This custard will not thicken very much, so remove from the heat as soon as you notice a slight change in texture. Stir in the sherry. Pour the mixture into a bowl to cool, and then refrigerate. Check after 1 hour.

As soon as the mixture becomes thick and syrupy, beat the heavy cream until soft peaks form and gently stir it into the custard. Cover the bowl with plastic wrap and chill at least 4 hours or longer before serving.

Apple-Walnut Pudding

(six servings)

This recipe originally called for dates, but in recent years we seem to have lost our taste for them. I think we have forgotten how splendid they are. Use apples or pears, but try dates sometime too.

1 cup all-purpose flour	2½ cups diced apples or pears
1 cup sugar	(cored and with skin on); or
2 teaspoons baking powder	1 cup pitted and chopped
½ teaspoon salt	dates
½ cup milk	1 cup chopped walnuts

Topping
2 cups boiling water   1 tablespoon butter
1 cup light brown sugar

Whipped cream

Preheat the oven to 350°F. Butter a 10 × 10 × 2-inch baking pan.

Put the flour, sugar, baking powder, and salt in a mixing bowl. Stir and mix well with a fork. Add the milk and briskly mix until smooth. Stir in the fruit and nuts. Spread the batter in the baking dish.

Put the water, brown sugar, and butter in a saucepan and bring to a boil, then pour the topping evenly over the batter. Bake, uncovered, for about 1 hour, or until the top is golden and bubbling. Serve with whipped cream.

Bread Pudding

(six servings)

This was a great pacifier for generations of boarding school pupils, since it would sometimes be the only decent dish on the menu. It is important to take it out of the oven while it is still trembling so it will be tender and soft rather than firm and dry. Serve with a little cream.

3 eggs	½ cup raisins
½ cup sugar	6 slices good home-style white
⅛ teaspoon salt	bread, crusts removed, but-
2½ cups milk	tered on one side
1½ teaspoons vanilla	

Preheat the oven to 350°F.

In a mixing bowl, stir together the eggs, sugar, and salt. Put the milk in a saucepan and heat over medium-high heat until the milk is scalded or tiny bubbles form around the edge of the pan. Remove the milk from the heat and slowly add the egg mixture, stirring constantly. Stir in the vanilla and raisins.

Place the bread, buttered sides up, in a 9-inch square baking dish. Pour the milk mixture over the bread. Put boiling water in a pan larger than the 9-inch baking dish and place in the oven. Put the baking dish in the larger pan, making sure the boiling water comes halfway up the side of the baking dish. Bake about 20 to 30 minutes, or until the custard is set. Serve warm.

Chocolate Pudding

(four servings)

This is the chocolate pudding of my childhood. As simple as a smile, it is creamy and smooth with a subdued chocolate flavor. It uses only two tablespoons of cocoa which give a light, delicate chocolate taste. Pour a tablespoon of heavy cream over each serving.

2 cups milk	2 tablespoons cocoa powder
3 tablespoons cornstarch	1 teaspoon vanilla
4 tablespoons sugar	Optional: 4 tablespoons heavy
¼ teaspoon salt	cream

Put 1½ cups of the milk in a heavy-bottomed saucepan and scald (this is the point of heat that is just short of boiling: there is steam rising from the milk and a ring of tiny bubbles around the edge). This is not critical; it is just that the milk should be very hot.

While the milk is heating, put the cornstarch, sugar, salt, and cocoa in a bowl. Stir with a spoon to mix, then add the remaining ½ cup cold milk, stirring until well blended. When the milk is hot, stir it into the cornstarch mixture and mix until well blended. Pour the mixture back into the saucepan and stir constantly until the pudding begins to boil. Boil *only 1 minute*, stirring briskly all the while. Remove from the heat and pour into a bowl. When cool add the vanilla. Cover and refrigerate until needed. Serve with a spoonful of heavy cream over each serving, if you wish.

Baked Vanilla Custard

(eight servings)

Baked custards are simple to make and always silkier, smoother, and more delicate than stirred custards.

2 egg yolks	3 cups very hot milk
3 eggs	1 tablespoon vanilla
½ cup sugar	Nutmeg
Salt to taste	

Preheat the oven to 325°F. Butter an 8-inch square baking dish or 8 ramekins. Set a shallow pan large enough to hold the baking dish or ramekins in the oven, and fill it with 1 inch of hot water.

Mix the yolks and eggs together until just blended. Stir in the sugar and salt and slowly add the hot milk, stirring constantly. Add the vanilla. Strain into the baking dish or ramekins and sprinkle with some nutmeg.

Put the dish or ramekins in the shallow pan and bake for about 45 minutes; the custard is set when a knife inserted in the center comes out clean. Be careful not to overbake; I remove custard from the oven when the very center still trembles a tiny bit.

Brown Sugar Custard

(six servings)

Brown Sugar Custard is rich and creamy. Serve it in small portions.

6 egg yolks	2 cups heavy cream
½ cup brown sugar	

Preheat the oven to 350°F. Butter a 9-inch pie plate.

Put the egg yolks, brown sugar, and cream in a bowl and beat until smooth. Pour into the buttered pie plate and bake for 20 minutes, or until the center is set. Cool and serve portions in individual dessert dishes.

Apples in Custard

(four servings)

The amazing thing about this recipe is that the apples get perfectly baked in just the same length of time it takes for the custard to set.

4 medium cooking apples, cored and peeled (Rome Beauty apples are best)	8 tablespoons sugar; plus 1 to 2 tablespoons for sprinkling

Custard

½ cup sugar	Salt to taste
2 cups milk	Optional: cream and maple
3 eggs	syrup
2½ tablespoons flour	

Preheat the oven to 350°F.

Place the peeled and cored apples in a square baking dish. Put 2 tablespoons of sugar in the center of each apple. Make the custard by mixing the ½ cup sugar, the milk, eggs, flour, and salt together. Pour over the apples and bake for 45 minutes, or until the custard is set.

At the end of the baking time, sprinkle the 1 to 2 tablespoons of sugar over the apples and custard, place under the broiler, and broil until lightly brown. Serve in individual bowls. You may put a small amount of cream and maple syrup over the top for additional flavor.

Wine Jelly

(eight servings)

This fine, no-fat dessert deserves the popularity it had a hundred years ago. It seems to me you need a little something that is slightly sweet to put a period at the close of supper, and wine jelly can do it.

2 envelopes unflavored gelatin	3 to 4 tablespoons freshly squeezed lemon juice
½ cup cold water	1 cup good sherry or Madeira
1⅔ cups hot water	wine
1 cup sugar	

In a small bowl, sprinkle the gelatin over the ½ cup cold water. Stir and let stand for 5 minutes.

Put the hot water and sugar in a saucepan and bring to a boil. Stir until the sugar dissolves. Remove from the heat and add the gelatin mixture; stir until it has dissolved. Add the lemon juice and wine, then taste, and add a little more lemon juice if it seems blah. Pour into individual dessert glasses or one pretty glass dish. Refrigerate until firm, about 2 hours.

Pralines

(thirty 2-inch round pralines)

Because candymaking at home has all but disappeared along with butter churning and preserving, no one thinks of making pralines anymore. These slightly grainy brown sugar pecan candies are so good, I wish I could get everyone to try these just once.

2⅓ cups *light* brown sugar
1 cup heavy cream
¼ teaspoon salt

2 cups coarsely chopped
pecans or walnuts

Put the sugar, cream, and salt in a 3-quart or larger heavy-bottomed saucepan. Turn the heat to medium, stirring the syrup until the sugar has dissolved. It will now take 15 to 20 minutes to finish cooking. Let the syrup come to a boil, without stirring. The mixture will boil up, becoming foamy with large bubbles, but it will soon settle down and the bubbles will become smaller and the foam will subside. Cook until the mixture reaches 238°F on a candy thermometer, or until it reaches the soft-ball stage. Start testing after 10 to 12 minutes. I prefer the soft-ball test because it is easy and it doesn't require a thermometer This is how it works: have a small cup of cold water near the cooking syrup, spoon out about ½ teaspoon of syrup, and drop it into the cold water. Gently roll the syrup between your fingers and if it holds together in a soft ball, it is ready to remove from the heat.

Have a long piece of waxed paper spread on the counter.

Remove the syrup from the heat and stir in the pecans; then stir briskly, for about 1 minute, but as soon as the syrup begins to look like it's getting firm, drop it onto the waxed paper. Drop the syrup by rounded tablespoonfuls onto the paper. Allow to cool completely, then remove from the paper and store in an airtight container between pieces of waxed paper. Or freeze.

Pineapple Blizzard

(four servings)

Abby Mandel, an exceptional cook and cookbook author, first made this dessert for me. I call it a "blizzard" because it is icy and it drifts up the sides of the food processor like wind-blown snow. It is creamy without cream and it keeps its soft frozen texture in the freezer.

4 cups fresh pineapple, cut into approximately 1-inch cubes
½ cup to ¾ cup sugar, depending on the sweetness of the pineapple

2 egg whites

Spread the pineapple cubes on a jelly-roll pan and put in the freezer for 8 hours. The cubes must be rock hard.

Put the cubes in the food processor and process until drifts of iced fruit are on the sides of the container (ignore the racket these little rocks make). This takes about 1 minute. Stop and scrape down the sides with a spatula, add some of the sugar, about ½ cup, and then add the egg whites. Process, stopping to scrape down the sides once or twice, until the mass begins to flow easily in the processor container. Process for 2 or 3 minutes, taste, and add more sugar if needed. Continue to process another 2 minutes, or as long as it takes for the mixture to become pale, light, and smooth. You will have the most creamy, fluffy pineapple dessert, and it will be difficult to believe that it only has sugar and egg white in it.

Cover well, and put into the freezer. This keeps for a week or two, but is at its best the first 3 or 4 days after making.

Grapefruit Ice

(four servings)

A glass of grapefruit juice is bracing at breakfast; turned into ice chips, it is my favorite fruit ice. With a few Plain Jane Sugar Cookies (see page 209) it makes a nice finish to almost any supper, but particularly one of Baltimore Crab Cakes (see page 59).

¾ to 1 cup sugar (depending on the tartness of the grapefruit juice)

½ cup water
3 cups grapefruit juice, freshly squeezed

Mix together the sugar and water in a saucepan and boil until the sugar is dissolved, about 1 minute. Cool, and stir in the grapefruit juice. Pour into ice cube trays (the smallest cubed trays are ideal because you can turn out a small dish of cubes for each serving). Or pour the juice mixture into a bowl. Cover and freeze. Remember to soften the ice a trifle so you can serve it easily if you are not freezing it in the tiny cubed ice trays. Serve in small glasses or bowls.

Chilled Marmalade Grapefruit

(four servings)

This is a short recipe that will win a long ovation. Icy cold, a little sour, and a little sweet, it goes with any plain cookie.

2 cups fresh grapefruit sec-   ¾ cup orange marmalade
tions (see page 197)

Put the grapefruit in a bowl and stir in the marmalade. Chill until very cold.

Sautéed Pears

(four servings)

The interesting thing about pears is that they are never ever robust—not even when they are raw and crunchy. Sautéed, they are at their delicate best, and are a welcome dessert after a rich dish such as Beef Stroganoff (see page 90). Serve warm with a little cream poured on top. These are also good with a sprinkle of finely chopped crystallized ginger.

4 tablespoons (½ stick) butter   ½ cup water
4 firm, ripe pears, peeled,   2 tablespoons dark brown
   halved, and cored   sugar

Melt the butter in a large skillet that has a lid, or in a sauté pan. Slice each pear half into quarters, add the slices to the pan, and slowly stir and turn for 1 minute. Add the water and stir in the brown sugar. Turn the heat to very low, cover, and let simmer for about 3 or 4 minutes. Check for doneness after 2 minutes, so the pears don't become too soft. They are done as soon as they are easily pierced with a fork. Remove from heat and serve warm.

Maple Persimmons

(one serving)

This Fuyu persimmon dessert is so good that you must try it once. Fuyu persimmons are the apple-shaped ones that can be eaten while still firm. (The acorn-shaped Hachiya persimmons must be very soft to be edible.) Maple syrup with cream and persimmons is a dessert to rave about.

1 Fuyu persimmon   2 tablespoons maple syrup
2 tablespoons heavy cream

Peel the persimmon and remove the core and seeds (sometimes only the seeds need to be removed). Cut into bite-size pieces and put in a dessert dish. Pour the heavy cream and maple syrup over the top. Serve chilled.

Grapes with Sour Cream and Brown Sugar

(four servings)

Brown sugar and sour cream melt together to make a light caramel sauce that turns an ordinary bunch of Thompson grapes into a fine dessert.

4 cups Thompson seedless grapes,   6 tablespoons light brown
   stemmed and washed   sugar
½ cup sour cream

Chill the grapes thoroughly in the refrigerator. Divide them among 4 dessert bowls, spread 2 tablespoons sour cream over each serving, and chill again. Thirty minutes before serving, sprinkle 1½ tablespoons brown sugar over each bowl of grapes, then return to the refrigerator. Of course, this can all be done in one bowl to be passed around the table.

Berry Sandwiches

(four servings)

When summer berries are sold all over the place, one of the simplest ways to serve them is to make berry sandwiches. It is essential to have a good fresh loaf of white bread.

4 cups berries (strawberries, blackberries, raspberries, any combination; strawberries hulled and sliced, other berries cleaned)

Sugar to taste (about 1 cup)
8 thin slices fresh white bread, crusts removed
1 cup heavy cream, sweetened lightly, whipped

Just before serving, spread the berries over 4 slices of bread. Put the other 4 slices of bread over the berries, and neatly spread the top and sides of the sandwiches with whipped cream. Garnish tops with a little swirl of berry juice. Slice each sandwich diagonally and place two halves on each serving plate.

Peach on Sugared Toast

(six servings)

Are you wondering why this is even a recipe? Because you may never have thought of it, and because it is actually better than some desserts that take a lot of fuss.

6 slices dense white bread,
  crusts removed
½ cup butter (1 stick), cut
  into 6 equal pieces

6 tablespoons sugar
3 large ripe peaches, halved
  and pitted
¾ cup heavy cream

Preheat the oven to 350°F. Butter a 9 × 13-inch baking dish.

Place the slices of bread in the baking dish. Spread each slice with a piece of the butter. Sprinkle 2 teaspoons of sugar over each slice of bread. Place a peach half, cut side down, on each slice and sprinkle 1 teaspoon of sugar over each peach half. Put the peaches in the oven and bake for 15 minutes. Remove, spoon 2 tablespoons of cream over each peach, and serve warm.

Baked Plums and Apricots
with Almonds

(six servings)

This French country dessert was served to me in Paris by Claudia Roden, the cosmopolitan food historian and cookbook author. Put it in the oven just before you sit down at the table, and it will come to the table bubbling hot for dessert. Serve with heavy cream or vanilla ice cream.

8 large apricots, halved and
pitted (about 2 pounds)
6 large plums, halved and
pitted (about 1 pound)
⅔ cup sugar plus 6 table-
spoons

⅔ cup water
1¼ cups whole unblanched
almonds

Preheat the oven to 325°F.

Put the apricots and plums in a large sauté pan. Stir the ⅔ cup sugar into the water, and pour into the pan. Cover and simmer over low heat for 5 to 7 minutes, or until the fruit is tender when pierced with a fork. Don't overcook. Set aside.

In a food processor, process the almonds and the remaining 6 tablespoons sugar until the mixture is very fine, but not a paste. Spread the mixture evenly in a 10-inch round baking dish. Arrange the fruit, cut side down, over the almond mixture. Pour ⅔ cup of the fruit juices remaining in the sauté pan over the fruit and almonds, and bake for 1 hour.

After baking, you may want to taste the fruit for sweetness. If

necessary, while the dessert is still hot, sprinkle more sugar on top.
Serve warm.

Baked Bananas with Berries
or Mango

(four servings)

There are people who have bunches of bananas in their kitchens
and who think they don't have anything for dessert, but a few of
those bananas plus a little coconut or some berries make a better
dessert than you can imagine.

1 tablespoon butter
4 firm ripe bananas, peeled
2 tablespoons lemon juice
4 tablespoons sugar
½ cup grated sweetened
    coconut

2 cups stemmed blueberries
    or diced mango, sweetened
    to taste

Preheat the oven to 375°F. Butter a baking dish approximately 8
inches square.

Put the bananas in the baking dish and evenly drizzle the lemon
juice over them. Sprinkle 1 tablespoon sugar over each banana, and
then sprinkle 2 tablespoons coconut over each. Bake the bananas
for 10 to 15 minutes, or until they are hot throughout. Remove
from the oven and place on serving dishes, arranging ½ cup berries
or diced mango over each serving. Serve while the bananas are hot.

Rhubarb and Kumquat Compote

(four servings)

This is unusual and wonderful—I found myself serving this repeatedly and no one got tired of it. Serve it with Almond Diamonds (see page 210) for a light supper dessert.

2 cups rhubarb, cut into
  ½-inch pieces
1 cup thinly sliced, seeded
  kumquats

¾ to 1 cup sugar
¼ cup water

Mix together the rhubarb, kumquats, ¾ cup sugar, and water in a saucepan. Cook over medium heat for about 5 minutes, or until the fruit is soft. Taste and add more sugar if necessary. Serve chilled, warm, or at room temperature.

SUPPER READINGS

When my son and daughter were about ten and twelve, I decided it would be a good idea to have the whole family read aloud at the table after supper. Actually, I first tried to persuade the children that memorizing poetry could be fun. The Victorians taught their children to memorize sentimental verses and recite these "memory gems" on special occasions. This sounded like a good exercise for young minds, but the children didn't cooperate and we didn't end up with any gems here. Next I proposed spending fifteen to twenty minutes each evening reading aloud at the table. At first there was more grumbling than reading, but somehow we managed to stick to the regime and even came to look forward to it. We read some classics, such as works of Mark Twain; and we read humor and nonsense by James Thurber and Ogden Nash. We read everything from Dr. Schweitzer to Dr. Seuss. Supper readings didn't make the children more obedient, helpful, or cheerful, but I'm glad we did it. We stayed together a little longer at the supper table, and I remember those times with pleasure.

Seasonal Supper Menus

SPRING

Asparagus Salad

Deviled Eggs

Lil's Ice-Water Crackers

Rhubarb and Kumquat Compote

Sweet Walnuts and Prawns

Jasmine Rice

Pineapple Blizzards

Salmon with Cucumber and Caper Sauce

Orzo with Fresh Dill

Sharon's Orange Scone Berry Cakes

SUMMER

Theater Steak

Fire and Ice Relish

Spanish Cream

Buffalo Chicken Wing Salad

Joyce's Almond Cakes with Berries

Eggs, Tomatoes, and Potatoes with *Gremolata*

Garlic Rolls

Grapes with Sour Cream and Brown Sugar

FALL

Posole Salad Soup

Sharp Cheddar Biscuits

Baked Plums and Apricots with Almonds

Southern Green Beans

Crouton Salad

Maple Persimmons

Chinese Hot and Sour Soup

Lil's Ice-Water Crackers

Baked Bananas with Berries

WINTER

Winter Vegetable Cobbler

Warm Applesauce and Crisp Ginger Cookies

Mustard Green Soup

Buttermilk Cornbread

Wine Jelly

Papusas

L.A. Slaw

Chocolate Pudding

Index

A NOTE ABOUT THE AUTHOR

Marion Cunningham was born in Southern California and now lives in Walnut Creek. She was responsible for the complete revision of *The Fannie Farmer Cookbook* and is the author of *The Fannie Farmer Baking Book* and *The Breakfast Book*. She travels frequently throughout the country giving cooking demonstrations, has contributed articles to *Bon Appétit, Food & Wine,* and *Gourmet* magazines, and writes a column for the San Francisco *Chronicle* and the Los Angeles *Times*. She has also been a consultant to a number of well-known West Coast restaurants.